For the
Love of Julie

For the Love of Julie

A nightmare come true.
A mother's courage. A desperate fight for justice.

ANN MING
with Andrew Crofts

HARPER
element

HarperElement
An Imprint of HarperCollins*Publishers*
77–85 Fulham Palace Road,
Hammersmith, London W6 8JB

www.harpercollins.co.uk

and *HarperElement* are trademarks
of HarperCollins*Publishers* Ltd

First published by HarperElement 2008

1

A catalogue record of this book
is available from the British Library

ISBN-13 978-0-00-726262-5 (hardback)
ISBN-10 0-00-726262-0 (hardback)
ISBN-13 978-0-00-726263-2 (paperback)
ISBN-10 0-00-726263-9 (paperback)

Printed and bound in Great Britain by
Clays Ltd, St Ives plc

Mixed Sources
Product group from well-managed
forests and other controlled sources
www.fsc.org   Cert no. SW-COC-1806
© 1996 Forest Stewardship Council
FSC

'It is one of those tales about how life can turn on a sixpence: one minute everything is dandy, the next all is darkness.'

Joe Joseph, *The Times,* 22 May 2002

Introduction

My daughter Julie was a funny mixture of introvert and extrovert. She was shy as a child but could be feisty in arguments when she thought she was in the right, and she didn't let anyone walk over her. She was hopelessly messy at home, dropping clothes where she took them off and leaving teacups lying around – but she never stepped out of the house without being perfectly groomed. She wouldn't want to be the centre of attention in a crowd, but around those she loved she never stopped talking, telling us anything and everything that was going through her head.

Julie was beautiful from the day she was born, with a slight oriental look from her Dad's side of the family, and dark colouring that let her get away with wearing the most dazzling bright colours. As a little girl she loved dressing her Sindy dolls for hours on end, and in her teens it was herself she dressed up. She'd wear ridiculously high heels, super-tight skirts and trousers showing off her perfect, slim figure, and eccentric shirts and jackets all layered on top of each other. Her hairstyle changed from month to month, but whether it was Boy George dreadlocks wrapped in rags, or a bright turquoise fringe, nothing fazed me. No matter how flamboyant an outfit she put together, she always looked stunning.

Julie had a dry (some would say warped!) sense of humour and an infectious giggle that bubbled out at inappropriate moments. She liked dancing, gymnastics and doing people's hair for them. She was a fantastic mother to her little boy Kevin, and fiercely loyal to her family and her close circle of good friends.

She was full of life and always fun to be with. She was my little girl and I adored her.

Chapter One

Julie's Arrival

In Middlesborough in the late 1960s it was the custom for mothers who had had one straightforward birth in hospital to deliver their babies at home after that, which is a daunting prospect for anyone, even for someone like me who prides herself on being a down-to-earth Yorkshirewoman. So many different fears and thoughts are racing through your head as your due date draws near. What if something goes wrong? What if the baby comes early, or gets stuck? When a newborn baby's life could be at stake it is very comforting to know you have all the technology and expertise of a well-equipped hospital at your disposal, rather than one midwife, a panicking husband and a pan full of boiling water. That option, however, was not on offer to us.

My mind was buzzing with fears of imagined disasters and imminent emergency ambulance rides as the pain started to build up. My mam took my two-year-old son Gary off for a walk in his pushchair to keep him out of the way. The midwife had popped in when the contractions started in the morning but then disappeared off, breezily saying she would be back at lunchtime, leaving my husband, Charlie, plenty of time to panic as my moans increased in frequency and he started to imagine having to perform the delivery himself. No doubt the midwife had plenty of other patients to tend to; for her it was just another day's work, even if it meant a lot more to us.

By eleven o'clock I had to go upstairs and lie down, hauling myself up on the banister, memories of just how painful the whole childbirth business is coming rushing back with every spasm. How is it that we women manage to forget all that agony almost the moment it is over? I could hear Charlie making frantic phone calls downstairs as I concentrated on the pain upstairs, lying on the bed, wanting it all to be over but not wanting the baby to come before the midwife got back.

The girl answering the phone at the doctor's surgery must have asked Charlie if I was starting to push.

'Are yer starting to push?' he shouted up.

'No,' I yelled back.

'Well, if the baby's born,' the girl told him, 'just wrap it in a blanket, wipe its eyes and put it on the side. Don't try to cut the cord.'

'This is good,' I heard him grumbling as he put the phone down. 'I pay me National Health stamps and there's nobody here when you need them!'

The doctor sauntered in at about twelve to take a look and immediately saw that I was ready to deliver whether the midwife was there or not.

'I'd better go and wash my hands,' he said, but just then the midwife bustled back in and he decided to go downstairs to keep Charlie company instead.

'I'll wait around in case you need stitches afterwards,' he said.

I dare say the two men were brewing up for a cup of tea as we women got down to work in the bedroom.

The birth itself was blissful and peaceful. 'She's arrived like an angel!' exclaimed the midwife, as Julie emerged into the world with her arms folded beatifically across her chest. That was the first I knew I had a girl, because of course we didn't have scans that could tell you in those days.

I hauled myself up on my elbows to catch a glimpse of my new daughter.

'My goodness,' the midwife marvelled, 'I've never seen a baby with so much hair.'

She was right: a thick mop of blue-black hair stretched down the back of the new baby's neck, a clear sign of her Chinese ancestry.

'She'll probably lose it all over the next few weeks,' she said, 'before she grows it back in again.'

But she didn't lose it. Julie's hair just grew thicker and darker and more lustrous with every passing week. The midwife, who became a regular visitor and friend over the following years, had to cut it after a month to let some air get to her little neck, pushing a hair slide into the side to keep it out of her eyes at an age when most babies have no more than a few tufts of fluff for a mother to brush lovingly.

I needed a few stitches after the delivery so Charlie was sent back to the kitchen to boil some needles for the doctor in a pan of water that he'd been preparing to cook some vegetables in for our lunch.

It was a Wednesday, 22 February 1967. 'Wednesday's child is full of woe', as the saying goes, which is what we used to say to Julie later whenever she was moaning at us about something or other. We could never have imagined how prophetic that silly little saying would turn out to be as we went about building our family life just like everyone else. None of us can ever know what lies in store for us, which is just as well.

As I lay in bed that afternoon, holding her in my arms for the first time, I never for a second would have believed that this tiny, helpless baby would die before I did, or that she would die in one of the most terrible ways possible. Such a thought would have been simply unbearable. At that moment my maternal instincts were to protect this vulnerable little bundle from everything life would throw at her – but it was an illusion because no mother can ever really hope to do that.

When your children are small you keep an eye on them most of the time, although even then accidents can still happen or terrible luck can befall them. But once they have grown up and left the nest you can do nothing but have faith that they will be all right, that they will not take too many risks or make too many bad judgements. And then all you can do is be there for them if things go wrong. But no matter how grown up and capable they become, I don't think a mother ever loses that initial instinct to guard her babies and fight for their safety and their rights against the rest of the world. Thankfully, not many have to do it in such horrific circumstances as I would have to.

Chapter Two

Meeting Charlie Ming

I first spotted Charlie Ming in 1962, sitting with a group of other men in a Chinese restaurant in Middlesborough called The Red Sun. I was just sixteen but had been out of school for a year and was more than ready for a bit of life. It was an exciting place for a young girl to be because there weren't many Chinese restaurants around in those days, not like today when there are fast-food outlets of every nationality on every street corner. In fact most people didn't eat out much at all; we didn't have anything like the amount of disposable money they have today.

Everything going on around me seemed exotic and foreign, including the men at the nearby table and especially Charlie. I couldn't tell how old he was, but it certainly wouldn't have occurred to me that he was twenty years older than me. I'm not sure I gave the question any thought at all. I'd never met a Chinese man before – not many people in our area had. They were still a rarity and viewed by most people with considerable suspicion. These were the days before any of us knew anything about race relations acts or the rules of political correctness; people still clung to their comforting prejudices and spoke their minds to the point of rudeness.

It all seems a bit like ancient history now, even though it was only forty-six years ago. This was the year when a young Nelson Mandela had only just been arrested and imprisoned in South Africa and when Marilyn Monroe was found dead under suspicious circumstances in her Hollywood apartment. It had also just become the Chinese year of the Tiger, traditionally said to be a volatile year in which there is likely to be massive change. There certainly was for me!

I'd been invited to the restaurant that night because a friend of mine was going out with one of the waiters and wanted me to go along with her for moral support. I'd been keen to accept the invitation, wanting to have a look at him. Boyfriends were still a very new experience for both of us, objects of considerable mystery and curiosity.

The group of Chinese men who had caught my eye were sitting in the corner, at a table that was almost next to ours, and I had a good view of them from where I was seated. To my young, inexperienced eyes they all looked the same, except for Charlie. There was something about him that caught my attention, and kept drawing it back. Apart from anything else, he was very good-looking.

'Who's that?' I asked my friend's boyfriend as he hovered round the table, bringing us food and flirting a little nervously at the same time.

'That's Charlie,' he told me. 'His mother's English and his father's Chinese.'

'Not a bad result when you mix them,' I said cheerfully, and probably quite loudly, assuming that none of this foreign-looking bunch of men would be able to speak English.

'Oh, thanks very much,' Charlie piped up in a thick Yorkshire accent, bringing the blood rushing to my face.

'You speak English?' I asked, shocked.

'I should hope so.' He grinned at my discomfort.

From that moment I was hooked, fascinated by someone who looked so mysterious and oriental but sounded so down to earth. As I got to know him and we told one another about our families, I found out his father had been the first Chinese man to come to the Middlesborough area, having travelled over from China to Birkenhead as a ship's steward in the days before air travel. It sounded like something from the movies, suggesting worlds beyond anything that my friends or I had ever experienced, or could even imagine. None of us had ever travelled outside our own hometowns, let alone gone abroad.

When he came ashore, Charlie's dad met an English girl, married her and decided to stay. He set up his own Chinese laundry, something that Chinese immigrants were doing all over the world in the first part of the twentieth century. It must have been a good business to be in then, despite the heat and the steam of the working conditions, in the days before washing machines or laundrettes had been invented.

Before long-distance travel became common, people were still very ignorant about foreigners and frightened of the myths and tales they heard circulating about Chinese men. Charlie told me about customers coming to the door with their laundry, or with their tickets and their money, and refusing to step any further inside for fear of being abducted or having their throats slit.

'You can come in,' he would tease them once he was old enough to start working there himself. 'We've not got any knives.'

He'd had a few troubles at school. He didn't really belong to either nationality – English or Chinese – so he was always the outsider, watching and smiling patiently, learning to be philosophical about life. It was a difficult upbringing that stood him in good stead for what life held in store for all of us. Charlie never expected life to be easy and he knew that you had to stick up for yourself or other people would walk all over you.

There was an immediate spark between us that night and he asked me out on a date. Unlike boys my own age, he had a car and on that first date he drove me over to Whitby for a day out. After I'd been out with him a couple of times I didn't think any more about his Chinese origins than I did about the age gap between us. He was just Charlie, the man for me. But other people didn't adapt quite so quickly.

I'd been born and brought up in Billingham, which was then not much more than a village on the outskirts of Middlesborough. Nothing much happened in Billingham apart from the giant ICI chemical works, which covered several hundred acres at the side of the town. The factory had originally been built during the First World War to produce the ingredients needed for the manufacture of explosives. It grew even larger during the Second World War and even in the 1960s it still provided most of the employment in the area, giving jobs to thousands of locals.

It's hard to imagine when you look at the wastelands around Billingham now just what a huge factory complex it once was, dominating the landscape for miles around with its gleaming towers and chimneys, belching smoke and steam, all part of the 'white heat of technology' that politicians liked to talk about in the 1960s.

No one back then could have predicted just how much the world was going to change for all of us with the arrival of the internet, global warming and so forth.

There were still virtually no oriental faces to be seen in this traditional industrial community, so Charlie and I got our fair share of racial abuse in the street when we were out together. A lot of people couldn't cope with the sight of a mixed-race couple and didn't hesitate to say so as they passed by, unbothered whether we heard or not. It was as if they thought girls like my friend and me were letting them down in some way by 'consorting with the enemy'. I can only imagine how much trouble Charlie's mam must have gone through when she married the very first Chinaman in the area back in the 1920s. She must have had a lot of guts.

My dad was one of the many thousands of men working at the ICI plant as a research chemist, but he died very suddenly at the age of sixty-two after having a massive brain haemorrhage while coming home from work on the bus. I was only fifteen at the time – this was shortly before I met Charlie – and I was completely devastated. It was such a shock because he hadn't been ill at all; it came right out of the blue. Dad had always pampered me and I idolized him. I was an only child and he and Mum had adopted me as a baby, but neither of them ever let me feel for a moment that I wasn't their daughter. They were always happy to do anything I asked. Dad and I never used to argue about anything. I couldn't even boil an egg by the time he died because he would insist on doing everything for me. Maybe that was why I was attracted to an older man like Charlie – especially one who was happy to do all the cooking.

Dad had looked after Mam well, too. She had never had a job outside the house that I could remember, had never written a cheque or paid a bill herself; he took care of everything like that. I think most men of that generation did in those days. Dad was the brainy one of the partnership.

Once he'd gone I automatically took on the role of doing all these practical things for her, even though I was still only fifteen years old, which meant I had to grow up a lot quicker than I would have done otherwise. That part of it didn't worry me. I just got on with things, but I still missed him terribly.

I didn't tell my mother about Charlie for a while, knowing that she was going to find it a bit difficult to get used to. It wasn't until a few months after I first went out with him that we were spotted together in Middlesborough by a friend of the family, who gleefully reported the news back to Mam. She went just as mad when I got home as I had imagined she would.

'You've been seen in Middlesborough with a Chinaman,' she announced the moment I walked through the door. 'Your father would turn in his grave. You know what's going to happen to you, don't you? He'll get you on a slow boat to China and he'll fill you full of opium. I'll tell you something else, they breed like rabbits and they're full of T.B.!'

There'd been an outbreak of tuberculosis (a deadly infectious disease that attacks the lungs and central nervous system) in Hong Kong a few years before, and this had been added to all the myths and prejudices that surrounded everything to do with the Chinese. The fact that Charlie had never been outside Yorkshire in his life didn't seem to make any difference to Mam's fears about disease-carrying foreigners who she imagined pouring off the boats like rats. People always like to gossip and to frighten one another with shocking tales of doom and gloom, and immigrants who look and sound different are always a good source of material. Mam had never got out much, always staying at home and looking after the house, so it was easy for the outside world to worry her.

Although I got on well with Mam and Dad, I became a bit of a rebel when I reached my teens, and I knew my own mind right from the start. I was never too bothered about conforming to other people's ideas of what I should or shouldn't do if it didn't suit me. When it came to choosing the man I wanted to be with I certainly wasn't going to take any notice of anyone else's prejudices. By the time Mam found out about us I already knew Charlie was a good catch and I wasn't going to give him up just to please her and a few neighbours who might disapprove of a mixed marriage. I didn't argue with her all that much; I just took no notice of her dire warnings and carried on with my life as if she hadn't said a thing.

'Well, you might as well bring him home then,' she huffed eventually, once she realized I wasn't going to change my mind no matter how black a picture she painted of the future I was choosing, or how often she pointed out the danger I was putting myself in by consorting with a 'foreign devil'.

Of course, the moment she met him Charlie worked the same gruff, twinkly charm on her that he had on me and a year later we got married, by which time Charlie was looking on her as a second mother and she couldn't praise him highly enough. He was always happy to do any odd jobs she needed doing, he'd include her without being asked when we were going on holiday or for a day out somewhere, and I'd sometimes arrive at her house to find he'd popped in for a coffee and a chat with her.

'I couldn't wish for a better son-in-law,' she would tell her friends at every opportunity, cutting off their prejudices before they could even leave their lips.

If I ever grumbled to her about anything Charlie had said or done she would immediately jump to his defence, making it clear she believed I was lucky to have landed such a good catch and that I should be grateful. Although it sometimes felt as though they were ganging up on me, I was relieved that we all got on well because if you can't keep your immediate family together around you, what hope do you have of leading a truly happy life? I've always believed that immediate family is the most important thing for anyone. Perhaps knowing that I was adopted and feeling lucky at being taken in by two such loving parents had a big effect on my thinking, making me more appreciative than other people who might take such things for granted.

It was Charlie who wanted to get married and start a family quickly because he was already in his late thirties. He wanted to have children while he was still young enough to enjoy them and I was quite happy to go along with him, thinking there would be plenty of time for me to work and have a life of my own later, once the children were off at school and didn't need me to be at home with them all the time.

We only had about twelve people at the wedding, which made it feel more like the Last Supper, because none of my other relatives were speaking to me, even though they knew Mam was now perfectly happy about the match. I wasn't too bothered. If they felt like that I didn't want anything to do with them anyway.

It wasn't just the family who didn't like the idea of a mixed marriage. When we bought our first house in Acklam, a nice area outside Middlesbrough, the next-door neighbour almost immediately got together a petition to persuade us to move straight back out again. The first I knew of it was when she turned up on the doorstep with a letter that she had persuaded five of the other neighbours to sign. It was a shock because I'd thought we were all getting on very well whenever we talked face to face.

'I've noticed,' she said, sounding a bit surprised, 'how clean you are. We don't mind you, but it's when your husband's friends come to visit that it lowers the tone of the area.'

Shocked, since I had always found Charlie's friends very pleasant, I told Charlie I thought we should move after that, not wanting to live somewhere there was an atmosphere and where we weren't wanted, but he wasn't having any of it.

'No.' He was adamant. 'We're staying here.'

When I thought about it I realized he was right. Who was to say the next set of neighbours wouldn't be even more hostile? We couldn't allow them to bully us like that so we took the petition to show to a solicitor and asked his advice. He wrote to all the neighbours who had signed it, pointing out the error of their ways. I guess they hadn't had their hearts in it – maybe they had just done it to please the woman next door – because they all apologized after that, even her. Perhaps they hadn't expected us to respond in that way, assuming we would just pack up and scurry off into the night. Ordinary people were still easily intimidated by official-looking letters from lawyers. Like all potential bullies, their resolve crumbled as soon as they saw we were going to fight back and not simply do as they told us. So Charlie was right to stand up for himself because everything settled down after that and we went back to being normal neighbours.

The political atmosphere has changed so much since then. If someone got together a petition like that these days, I imagine it would be all over the front pages of the papers and there would be questions in Parliament. It was really just a question of sticking up for ourselves, something we would become very good at over the years.

In the end I got used to people who didn't know him talking to Charlie in Pidgin English, as if he was just off the boat. I even managed to see the funny side sometimes. 'What pricey you likey?' someone at a cinema ticket desk would shout at him helpfully, and sometimes Charlie would play along with them, looking vacant as if he couldn't understand a word they were saying. I couldn't really be too indignant since I had made almost exactly the same mistake when I first met him.

We had our first child, Gary, in 1965, a couple of years after we married, by which time I'd just turned nineteen.

'What colour's Ann's baby?' our next-door neighbour asked Ellen, a friend of mine.

'He's green,' Ellen replied, with a straight face.

Julie came along in 1967 and then Angela made her appearance in 1969. With three small children running around, the house was soon too small for us all and we put it up for sale. The woman who had organized the petition when we first moved in asked me how much we were asking for it.

'That depends,' I replied.

'Depends on what?'

'Depends on the colour of the buyer's skin,' I said. 'The darker they are, the cheaper they can have the house.'

Although I was only joking we did end up selling to a man who had a half African wife, so that probably confirmed the neighbour's worst fears about how the neighbourhood had now gone completely to pot. Times were changing in so many different ways.

Chapter Three

Family Life

Once we had found a buyer for our first home in Acklam we moved round the corner to a bigger house, where we stayed while the children grew up, creating a happy stable family base.

Gary was always the mischief-maker amongst the three children and Angela took after me, brimming with confidence and plenty to say for herself on all occasions. Julie was the quietest, shyest one of the bunch. She wasn't as outgoing as her brother or sister and didn't make friends quite as easily. It wasn't as if she didn't have friends, but they were a small, select group rather than a big crowd. Once someone had become her friend she tended to keep them in her life for a long time.

As she grew up she looked a lot like the few pictures we had of Charlie's English mam, although her pretty, almond-shaped eyes gave a hint of the oriental blood that flowed in her veins, showing she was definitely a member of the 'Ming dynasty'.

Charlie worked for Shell as a 'heavy goods fitter', which is another way of saying he was a mechanic working on their lorries. He worked hard and was a good provider, but bringing up three children is never going to be cheap. From soon after Julie was born, I worked on Friday and Saturday nights at the cash desk of a local Chinese restaurant in Billingham. The restaurant was owned by one of Charlie's friends and they used to get quite a few actors and performers coming in from the nearby theatre after the shows finished. (We didn't call them celebrities then, although I guess they were because they were usually off the telly.) I'd first gone to the restaurant to help them out for a week and ended up staying there for fifteen years, mainly because I enjoyed the buzz of the place.

Once Angela reached the age of five and started at school I found I had a bit of time on my hands so I got myself a job at the local hospital as an auxiliary nurse, to earn us a bit of extra money and to keep myself busy. I was lucky that my mam could look after the kids while I did my shifts – usually twelve till nine – and Charlie took over when he got in. I had never wanted to live a life like Mam's with no outside interests beyond home and family and I'd always liked the idea of being a nurse, even when I was a little girl. Meeting Charlie and starting a family had only temporarily distracted me from doing something about it.

Once the hospital took me on I was very quickly working inside the operating theatre, doing a bit of everything. Despite having always thought that I wanted to be out on the wards, chatting to the patients, I loved the work and I soon got used to dealing with the temperamental surgeons, men who everyone used to treat as if they were gods. Hospital life was still very formal in those days with a strict hierarchy and no one on first-name terms or anything like that. The surgeons used to do a lot of shouting and none of us ever dared to answer them back; we were too busy running around to do their bidding as quickly as we could.

Julie was never any trouble to us or to her teachers at school when she was a child. She took up gymnastics and soon proved able to fold herself in two and make her body do all sorts of things that seemed impossible to me. She was a good dancer as well, being small and slightly built.

Of all our children she was the one who could always wrap Charlie round her little finger the easiest. If the others wanted anything they would tell her to go and ask him for it, knowing he could never refuse her anything. It was a bit like my relationship had been with my dad, I suppose. She was a proper daddy's girl and I think maybe he saw a bit of his mam in her.

We led a very normal, contented family life, with all the usual ups and downs, petty rows and reconciliations, family treats and family chores. Every year when the kids were young we used to go down to Devon or Cornwall for our holidays, always taking my mam with us. For seven or eight years in a row we hired a big caravan in Looe. Mam was always good for baby-sitting and for giving Charlie and me little breaks. On our final trip there, with Charlie's brother and his wife, we had fourteen days of solid rain and decided that next time we would go to Majorca for some guaranteed sun. Julie was eighteen by then and the highlight of the holiday for her was buying herself a white leather suit that she wore almost constantly once we got back. It looked terrific on her.

We used to go out as a family in the summer afternoons too, once Charlie had finished his shifts and the kids were home from school. I would ring Mam up and she would catch a bus over and join us for a run over the moors. All of us would pile into our old blue and white van, Mam sitting in state in the front with Charlie and the rest of us rattling around in the back with no seats. We even used to have the pram in with us when we still needed it. We took Mam everywhere we went because otherwise she would just have been sat at home on her own.

When the kids were in their teens, Charlie and I took the opportunity to travel to China with a couple of friends, leaving the kids with my mam. We spent a month in Hong Kong and then a week in Canton, where Charlie's dad had originally come from all those years before. In Hong Kong we stayed with Charlie's aunt in a village in the New Territories called Fan Ling, where I was the only European face to be seen in any direction and no one spoke any English. The streets bristled with life as people went about their daily business on bicycles and carts, and mah jong was being played on every corner.

Then we travelled to a village called Sha Tau Kok on the border with China, where a friend of ours lived. We had to get police permission in Hong Kong to get that close to the border. I stood out even more there and I got used to feeling like the Pied Piper of Hamelin, followed by a trail of curious kids wherever I went, everyone wanting to touch my blonde hair because they'd never seen anything like it before. When we walked into one busy, crowded restaurant every single person stopped eating and talking, turning as one to stare. It was a shock to see huge crowds of Chinese faces everywhere we went because I'd spent my whole life in Europe, never even thinking about what colour I was.

'Keep hold of me,' I warned Charlie when we first arrived, 'or I might lose you and end up going home with the wrong one.'

Obviously Chinese people don't 'all look the same' once you get to know them, any more than Europeans do, but when you are confronted by crowds of strangers it's very confusing. Charlie always says it's the same in reverse for him in Middlesborough.

My mother was living in a council bungalow in Billingham at that time and the rent kept going up every year, leaving her very short of cash.

'Why don't we buy the house as an investment?' Charlie suggested. 'Then your mam can live there rent free.'

At first the council refused to sell to us because they said the bungalow was supposed to be for old people, but I'd known the area a long time and knew that wasn't true, so I wrote to the Secretary of State in London and got the council overruled. I've never been willing to just accept what people tell me simply because they're in a position of authority, although at that stage I had no idea how far this stubborn streak in my nature would one day be tested.

We eventually bought the bungalow off the council in the April of 1980 but Mam had a stroke a couple of months later, which turned all our carefully laid plans upside down. She was still able to shuffle about on her feet once she'd recovered, but her brain never really worked properly after that and it was obvious she was going to be going steadily downhill over the coming years. We realized there was no way she was going to be able to look after herself much longer so we sold our house in Acklam, had Mam's bungalow extended and moved the whole family in there together. It was an easier option than trying to uproot her from her own house after so many years now that she was becoming frail.

Although I was worried about Mam and didn't know whether we would be able to look after her properly, I liked the idea of going back to Billingham, back to where all my roots lay. When you look back at the decisions you make in life you can't help but wonder how things would have gone if you had just followed a different path. How different it might all have been if we had moved Mam in to live with us in Acklam rather than the other way round. I can't help thinking that if we hadn't made that move our Julie would still be alive today.

If I had known how difficult looking after Mam was going to be I don't know if I would have had the courage to take on the job for those last few years. By the end she was incontinent and away with the fairies most of the time. The kids were always good at helping out with her; we couldn't have done it without their support. Angela was particularly good, willing to clean her up when she soiled herself and everything. Our Julie was a bit more squeamish; she would be willing to keep Mam company, feed her, curl her hair and generally entertain her for hours on end, but she didn't like the other stuff.

We developed a routine of caring. I had Mam during the week and went to work at the hospital at weekends, when Charlie and the girls would take over. Charlie never complained. In fact it was him who insisted that she stay with us and not be put in a home. She had done too much for both of us and for the children over the years for us to think of abandoning her to the mercies of strangers. So we soldiered on.

Mam continued to live with us until she died five years later in 1985. It was sad to lose her, obviously, but it was a relief too because she hadn't really been with us mentally for several years by that time yet she had needed looking after twenty-four hours a day. With Mam gone and the children growing up, Charlie and I thought that perhaps now life would get a bit easier for us. Shell decided to close the depot he worked for so he took early retirement. We had some money in the bank and a chance to stand back and think about what we wanted to do with the next part of our lives together. Charlie decided to invest some of his money in buying a catering trailer, serving drinks and snacks to passing motorists, which he set up in a lay-by on the A66 to Darlington.

We worked hard and we were proud of how we had brought up the kids. Now we felt we could relax a bit and enjoy ourselves. How wrong could we have been? It's just as well none of us could see into the future because if we had had any idea what was coming a few years down the line I don't know how we would have faced it.

Chapter Four

Our Julie Grows Up

When Julie was sixteen, just after leaving school, she met a Billingham boy called Andrew at a local youth club. She was the same age as I had been when I met Charlie but somehow she seemed much less mature than I had imagined I was at that age. Maybe we all kid ourselves that we are more grown up than we are when we first start to spread our wings.

Although she was never outgoing in a crowd, Julie was a bit of a rebel in the way she dressed, did her hair and made herself up. She always liked to wear weird clothes, often adopting fashions long before other people she knew would have had the nerve. At that time she was going through her Boy George phase, dressing like him and doing her hair the same way. She would get Angela to tie rags in it and then put a black hat on the top of the whole thing. She would pinch Charlie's white shirts and cut the collars off and wear black gloves and lots of eyeliner to go out in the evenings. Once she was out on the dance floor all her usual inhibitions seemed to vanish. It's strange how some people can be shy and introverted in some ways and extroverted in others. I suppose it's all part of what makes people different and interesting. When she was dancing she seemed to come into herself.

She liked to wear really high heels to try to make herself look taller, fed up about the fact that she was so much smaller than Gary and Angela. As a result she didn't always choose the most practical shoes for everyday life but that never worried her. I went into Middlesborough with her once when she had these bright orange high heels on.

'My feet are killing me,' she grumbled after we'd been walking round the shops for a bit. 'Will you swap, just for ten minutes, Mam?'

'Only ten minutes,' I said firmly.

What is it about being a mother that makes you willing to put yourself through agony rather than see one of your children in pain, even when they have inflicted it on themselves in the first place? A mixture of natural instincts and motherly love, I suppose. I was still wobbling along in these ridiculous bright orange stilettos when we bumped into someone from my work and I had to do some fast explaining.

When she left school, Julie started training as a hair-dresser. She had always been interested in messing around with her own hair, dying it shocking pinks and blues long before such colours were generally accepted, so it seemed like a good choice of career for her. Her hair was still incredibly thick, just as it had been when she was a baby, and when she permed it, it became even more spectacular. Big curly perms were all the fashion round our way in the 1980s, and Julie's was the biggest and curliest. When she came home with blue hair after my mother had had her third stroke, Mam was convinced it was a hat.

'What a lovely hat,' she kept saying. 'What a lovely colour.'

'It's not a hat, Mam,' I told her, 'it's her damned hair!'

Julie wanted to practise her hairdressing on everyone and she even persuaded her dad to have a perm in his dead-straight, coal-black Chinese hair. It actually didn't look too bad once she'd done it, so he kept it.

Charlie and I liked Andrew from the first time Julie brought him home. He was very relaxed about life and good at gently humouring her if she was in one of her moods. He was a couple of years older than her and working as a painter and decorator. Having been married for nearly twenty years to Charlie by then, who was a strong and sometimes controlling character, I could appreciate the attraction of being with a man who was a bit more easy-come, easy-go. Andrew just fitted into our family as if he had always been there.

In 1985, the year Mam died, Julie and Andrew got married and moved into a council house just down the road in Billingham, 27 Grange Avenue. It was only five minutes' drive away from us. I was very happy for them. I'd been born and brought up in the area myself and knew it well, so it felt as though Julie was staying close to her roots.

It was a lovely wedding and when I watched Julie and Andrew dancing to 'Ave Maria' at the reception I felt like the complete proud mum, happy to have brought up such a pretty girl and to be able to see her settling down with a nice man. 'Ave Maria' was her favourite song and she looked so beautiful and so joyful as they whirled around the dance floor that at that moment it didn't seem possible they wouldn't have a wonderful happy life together.

Even though Julie was now a married woman it often felt as though she hadn't left home at all. We would see her every day, and there would be phone calls from her all the time. Gary had left home and started work as a bricklayer and, even though Angela was still living with us, she was very independent and had just starting her training as a dental nurse. But our Julie wouldn't let go of the apron strings.

'Are you in, our Mam?' she would ring and ask at least once a day. 'I'll pop round then.'

She was nearly always round for her tea, because we usually had the sort of Chinese food the children had been brought up eating. Charlie had taught me how to cook it at the beginning of our marriage and we all thought of it as our staple diet. As a family we used chopsticks all the time without even thinking about it.

Sometimes she would come round for one of her daily visits, then go home and ring half an hour later, even though she didn't have anything new to say. She just liked to chat about nothing or about anything that had come into her head in the previous few minutes. Although I would get exasperated with her sometimes if I was trying to get on with doing something else, I wouldn't have had it any other way; I loved having her around. Even when I was at work she would be ringing all the time; the others in the operating theatre used to tease me about it every time another call came through.

'You've got to stop ringing me so much at the hospital,' I'd tell her every so often. 'You're going to get me into trouble.'

'Oh, aye,' she would reply, good-naturedly. 'I will.'

But she never did. The moment she thought of something to tell me or ask me she would be dialling again without a second thought.

My colleagues at the hospital were used to her ways, having known her since she was little. Because I worked weekends the kids often used to come in to see us when they were little, if we weren't busy. All the other staff knew them and they weren't nervous about the theatre or even the god-like surgeons.

Julie came into the hospital to see me one day when she was about seven months pregnant, the year after she and Andrew were married. There were just three of us on duty that day and nothing much was happening so we were able to pay her some attention.

'Get up on the table,' one of the other nurses told her. 'We'll get the stethoscope and see if we can hear the baby's heart beating.'

She was up on the table with her belly exposed while we tried to find the baby's heart when one of the surgeons, Mr Clark, suddenly burst into the room.

'What the bloody hell is going on in here?' he wanted to know.

'Our Julie's pregnant and we're trying to find the heartbeat,' I explained nervously.

'Oh, get out of the way,' he barked. 'I'll find it.'

Julie went bright red as he took over and found the heartbeat almost immediately. This same surgeon had been very generous when Julie was married, passing on a load of furniture that he and his wife didn't want to go in her new home. Everyone around the hospital was good to us like that, treating us like family.

When she was close to her due date both she and Andrew came to live with us for two weeks because she wanted to be at the heart of the family at such an important time. I guess maybe she still didn't feel ready to leave the nest even though she was a married woman and soon to be a mother. Andrew never seemed bothered about anything like that, always fitting in easily wherever he was, happy to go along with whatever Julie wanted.

The birth all went smoothly and Julie instantly took to motherhood. A few weeks after little Kevin had arrived she and I popped out to the off-licence to buy some chocolate, leaving the baby with Andrew and Charlie.

'I feel really strange,' she said once we were away from the house. 'This is the first time I've come out without Kevin since I had him.'

'I feel like that with you,' I told her, 'even though you're married now. I don't think a mother ever feels complete without her children around her.'

'Ah, Mam,' she teased, 'but I'm a woman now.'

'Yeah, I know, but I still feel the same about you.'

When the time came to take Kevin to the mother and toddler group Julie wanted me to go too.

'Ah, come on, our Mam,' she wheedled when I said I didn't think any of the other girls would be taking their mothers. 'I don't want to go on my own.'

She never liked to do things on her own and I never complained about being included because she was always a laugh to be with and I enjoyed her company. It was great to be invited to be such a big part of my grandson's early life.

Charlie and I were always very happy with Andrew as a son-in-law and to start with the marriage appeared to go well, especially once they had Kevin to look after. They were both so proud of him and so anxious to do the right things. But becoming a mother seemed to bring Julie a bit more out of her shell and after a couple of years things began to go wrong between them. I think it was mostly down to them both being so young and immature – she was just eighteen and he was only twenty when they married. Julie couldn't cook at all; the first time she put a chicken in the oven she left the plastic bag of giblets inside it. It's hard to sustain a marriage when neither of you know anything about life. I think they both thought it was all going to be a bed of roses, which it never is once you've got a small child. I was young too when I married and started having babies (and I couldn't cook either), but life was different then, people didn't have the same expectations, and at least Charlie was older and more experienced.

Andrew liked to go out playing football and snooker, like any young lad. That would make our Julie get all possessive and grumpy and they would end up arguing about stupid things. They were each just as bad as the other. There was one time when Andrew was obsessed with getting his car mended. Julie and I had been out shopping at Asda and when we got back we found he'd swapped their microwave for a particular engine part that he needed. She was furious, but she could be just as daft herself sometimes. She'd bought a lemon and grey striped pushchair for Kevin and one time she said she wasn't able to come out with me because his matching lemon suit wasn't dry from the wash and his others wouldn't have matched the pushchair's upholstery! They were both still just a couple of kids themselves really.

Andrew had been doing some work at a pizza place in Station Road in Billingham. Bizarrely, the shop, called 'Mr Macaroni', was owned by an Iranian family. Some time around 1987, Julie started working there as well, driving a pizza delivery van in the evenings to earn some extra money. Looking back, I suppose she and Andrew had less time together then and they started drifting apart.

Things must have been worse between them than Charlie and I realized because in 1989, when he got the chance of a job down in London with his uncle, Andrew decided to take it. They both seemed to see it as the first step in a separation. Charlie and I were very sad about it, but at least we were close by to help her with Kevin and we never felt that Andrew was to blame any more than she was for the fact that they were drifting apart. It was just one of those things that happen in families and you have to adjust and move on.

It looked as if Julie was going to be able to cope quite well on her own, with us in the background to help her. On the nights she was working late she would leave Kevin to sleep over with us. It was a good arrangement for all of us because Charlie and I liked having a child around the house and we liked feeling we were helping her. Julie would often work from about five in the afternoon until midnight. She enjoyed working with the Iranians, but I was told she never let them push her around. One friend told me she was in the queue in 'Mr Macaroni' one day when one of the owners was trying to boss Julie about.

'She just picked up the dough and dumped it on his head,' my friend told me.

They must have valued her as an employee because they didn't sack her, even then. I could just imagine her doing that and I liked the idea that she would stick up for herself.

Charlie and I had been thinking about what we should do now that the children were growing up. Once Gary and Julie had both moved out, and Angela was getting close to leaving, we decided we didn't need a house as big as Mam's old bungalow any more and we put it up for sale. It went really fast, selling before we'd had time to find anything else to buy, so we moved into a rented property while we sorted ourselves out and worked out where we would like to go next.

As the autumn of 1989 arrived I fancied a break. I've always liked going to Blackpool for holidays but Charlie doesn't much like the place, so I asked Julie if she would like to come with me for a few days away. We always had a laugh when we were together. Andrew said he would mind Kevin (he hadn't left for London by then) and we set off for some mother and daughter time. We hadn't even booked anything – you didn't have to at that time of year; we just turned up and found ourselves a bed and breakfast before setting out to enjoy the sights. Julie had always liked the fairgrounds, riding on the big dippers and all the rest, and I was happy to watch her, just as I had when they were all small children.

'I think I'll have me fortune told,' she said as we walked past a gypsy's stall in a shopping arcade. 'Do you want to come?'

'Oh, I'm not wasting my money,' I said. 'You go ahead.'

I wandered off, leaving her to it. She reappeared a few minutes later.

'That cost me five pounds,' she complained. 'She said I have a son who's going to be musical, but we all know Kevin's tone deaf, and after that she said she couldn't tell me anything else. It was like I didn't have any future.'

That Blackpool clairvoyant will never know how right she was with her predictions that day.

Chapter Five

Our Julie Goes Missing

On Thursday 16 November 1989, two months after our trip to Blackpool together and about a month after Andrew had gone down to London to work with his uncle, Julie was due to go to court in nearby Stockton to apply for a legal separation. I agreed to go with her, partly because we always did things like that together and partly because I thought she might need a bit of moral support. These sorts of legal procedures are always more emotional than you might expect them to be and I didn't like the idea of her having to face it on her own. At times like that I knew Julie preferred to have me around; it was just the way we did things.

'Andrew and me are not going to get back together, our Mam,' she told me when I asked if she was absolutely sure this was the route she wanted to follow. 'I've been to see a solicitor and he says it's best we make it official.'

Realizing she had made up her mind and there was nothing I could do but be supportive, I didn't say any more. She said she was going to be working the night before.

On the 15th, the afternoon before we were due to go to the court, I went down to her house to pick up Kevin just as I normally did when she was working late, making deliveries in the pizza van. She was double-checking all the arrangements as usual. She always got anxious about things like that.

'You won't forget to call me in the morning, will you, our Mam?' she said as Kevin and I were leaving the house. 'I have to be in court at ten, so we'll need to set out around nine. Ring me about half seven to make sure I'm awake.'

'Why don't you come and stay at home tonight?' I suggested. 'Then you can take your time in the morning.'

'No, I want to stay in my own house,' she said casually. 'Just don't forget to call me at seven-thirty.'

'Don't worry,' I said. 'I will, and I'll be down to get you about half eight.'

'You won't forget, will you?' she said.

'I won't,' I assured her, used to her always fussing like this about things like appointments.

How many thousands of times have I wished that I had kept on nagging her to come and stay with us that night? I'm sure I could have made her if I'd kept on at her for long enough, but it didn't seem worth arguing about at the time. She was a grown-up after all; it was perfectly reasonable that she would want to sleep in her own bed after a long evening's work. Part of me was always pleased when she showed a bit of independence anyway, and it meant we wouldn't be disturbed by her coming in late, so I said no more.

I'd just got back to our house with Kevin when the phone rang and I knew it would be her again, because it nearly always was.

'It's just me again, Mam,' she said. 'You won't forget to ring me in the morning, early, will you?'

'Stop worrying,' I grumbled. 'I'll be ringing you.'

That was the last time I heard her voice. There are so many things I wish I'd said in that call, but why would I have thought to say any of them since I expected to see her again in a little over twelve hours' time? I wish I could just have told her how much I loved her. I wish I could have said goodbye properly, but that isn't how things work. You can't go through life treating every phone call and every conversation as if it is going to be your last.

That night I didn't sleep well. I woke at ten past three, an odd time of night to wake. There was a horrible feeling of foreboding churning around inside my stomach, as if something bad was happening somewhere else, giving me premonitions. I told myself not to be stupid, that I must just have been having a bad dream or something, but still the feeling wouldn't go away and wouldn't allow me to get back to sleep. Small worries can grow like weeds in the darkest hours of the night and I hate lying in bed once I'm awake with my mind turning round and round, so I got up and tip-toed downstairs, being careful not to disturb Charlie, who was sleeping soundly.

If it had been an hour earlier I would have rung Julie to check she had got in all right from work, just to put my mind at rest, but I assumed she would be in bed by then and asleep. I didn't want to disturb her when she was going to have to be up early anyway. I made myself a cup of tea and eventually the feeling of dread in my stomach eased a little and I went back to bed for a few hours of fitful sleep until the alarm went off.

The next morning, I got Kevin up to give him his breakfast, then dead on seven-thirty I rang Julie's number as promised. When I got no reply I assumed she must be too deeply asleep after her late shift for the phone to penetrate her dreams. Muttering irritably to myself, I decided I'd better go down to wake her up in person. I carried Kevin out and strapped him into the car so we could drive down the road to Grange Avenue to wake his mam up and hurry her along.

As I parked and got out of the car I could see all the curtains were tightly closed upstairs and downstairs so I was pretty sure she was still fast asleep. Not expecting to be more than a couple of minutes, I left Kevin in the car and bustled up the front path. I didn't have a key so I knocked on the door, mildly exasperated with her for putting me to all this extra trouble. My knocking had no more effect than the phone call had, and I was aware I was making a lot of noise for any of the neighbours who might still be asleep. I tried calling through the letterbox a few times.

'Julie! Julie! Wake up. It's yer mam.'

I pressed my ear to the door to see if I could hear any sign of her stirring but everything inside remained deathly silent; no sound of sleepy footsteps on the stairs, no answering shouts from upstairs. I didn't want the whole street to know our business if I could help it so I went round to the back of the house to see if I would have better luck attracting her attention from there. I peered in through the kitchen window, knocked on the back door and called her name again a few times. Nothing like this had ever happened with Julie before and I was puzzled. She wasn't that deep a sleeper normally.

None of us had mobile phones in those days, although that seems hard to imagine nowadays given how much we all rely on them, so I decided to drive down to the main road where the phone box was to give it another go. Kevin was still in the car, apparently quite contented to be driven back and forth for a while without asking any questions. He was ever so patient for a three-year-old. Once I was in the phone box, watching Kevin in the car out of the corner of my eye, I dialled her number again, not sure what I would do next if she didn't pick up. The phone rang and rang. Still no answer.

I was beginning to think that maybe she wasn't in the house because it seemed unlikely the phone wouldn't wake her after so many tries. Maybe, I thought, she had gone to stay with a friend at the last minute. She was, after all, a grown woman and might have met someone during the evening and decided to go home with them, although it did seem very out of character. But why wouldn't she have rung to tell me where she would be? She had been so insistent about me ringing to wake her at seven-thirty, surely she wouldn't have forgotten so easily? And why would the curtains all be so firmly drawn if she wasn't in there? Maybe, I told myself, she had drawn them before she went out. Perhaps she had fallen asleep somewhere else and just didn't realize the time, parked up somewhere in her van maybe. All these possibilities were going through my head, but none of them seemed very likely. There just wasn't any explanation I could think of that seemed like the sort of thing Julie would do.

I drove back down to the house, with Kevin still chattering happily in his car seat, and tried knocking and shouting through the letterbox a few more times before I noticed a man over the road watching me from his window. I went across to talk to him.

'Have you seen our Julie?' I asked.

'No,' he said. 'Actually, I didn't even hear her coming back last night. I normally hear her coming in around one-thirty when she's working, being dropped off by someone. I don't remember hearing anything last night.'

You can't usually keep much secret in a small street like Grange Avenue where so many of the windows overlook the road and night-time noises travel easily up to people's bedrooms.

Trying not to panic or think the worst, I drove back down to the phone box once again and called a couple of her friends in case one of them had seen her or heard from her, or in case she had gone round to one of their houses unexpectedly for some reason. None of them had seen her or had any suggestion where she might be. They were as puzzled as I was. I wanted to ring the Iranians from the pizza shop to find out whether they could tell me if she had gone home after her shift, but I knew they didn't live on the premises and I had no other number or address for them. The shop wouldn't be open for hours yet so I knew there would be no point driving round there.

I went back again to bang on the door some more, unable to think of anything else to do. Kath, the woman who lived next door, came out to see what was going on.

'I can't raise our Julie,' I told her. 'Have you heard anything in the night?'

'I never heard anything at all,' Kath said.

By this time there was a feeling growing in my guts that something was seriously wrong, but I had to keep calm because I still had Kevin in the car and I didn't want to alarm him. There just didn't seem to be any logical reason why Julie wouldn't be in the house or why she wouldn't respond to my calls and shouts. I couldn't work out what was going on and that was frightening me. I wanted to share my worries with someone else in the family, hoping they would tell me I was being stupid and that there was an obvious explanation.

I knew Gary was working as a brickie on a job nearby in Billingham, so I drove to the site to see if he had come in yet. More than anything I just wanted someone else to be with me while I tried to work out what was going on and what I should do about it. He was there when I drew up outside the site, and was obviously surprised to see me.

'What's up, our Mam?' he asked.

'I don't know where our Julie is,' I blurted as soon as I saw him.

'She phoned last night asking me over,' he said, 'but I didn't get in on time. I haven't heard since.'

His boss could see how worried I was and told Gary to go with me and sort it out; he said he could manage without him for a couple of hours. We drove back to Julie's house together. Nothing had changed. The curtains were still tightly drawn, no sign of life anywhere. We went round to the back once more and I took Kevin with me this time, not wanting to leave him in the car on his own now that the street was waking up and there were more people around. We knocked and shouted and peered in the windows again, but there was no sign of life inside.

'I need to get in,' Gary said, now obviously sharing my anxiety. 'We'll have to break something.'

There was a narrow panel of glass beside the back door, which Gary smashed and climbed through after pulling out the remaining shards of glass. I could see there was no way I was going to be able to get through such a small gap.

'Go round the front,' he told me, 'and I'll find the keys and let you in.'

I hurried back to the front door, clutching Kevin and trying to answer his stream of questions about why his uncle had just smashed his way into his mam's house, even though my mind was miles away, racing over a hundred different scenarios, each one worse than the one before. I was struggling to keep my rising panic under control. The front door was still shut when I got there and I waited for Gary to open it. Nothing happened for what seemed to me like an age.

'What's going on, Gary?' I shouted, no longer caring who I might wake up. 'Open the door!'

A few moments later he pulled back the curtains in the front room and opened the window to talk to me. 'There's no keys in here, Mam,' he said. 'I'm just going to look upstairs.'

I stood at the window, my heart thumping in my chest as he disappeared off to search the rest of the house. He was back a few minutes later although it seemed like hours.

'There's something wrong in here, Mam,' he said, his face serious. 'Everywhere's tidy. The bed's all made and the kitchen's been cleared, everything's been put away neatly. There's no sign of our Julie anywhere.'

Julie had always been untidy and when she got out of bed in the morning she would throw the duvet back and leave it like that until she was ready to get back into it again at night, then she would just shake it out and throw it back over herself. It was her routine and had been for years. Why would she do it all differently today? When she washed up in the kitchen she would always leave the stuff out to drain on a rack; she never dried things up and put them away. Being in a bit of a mess didn't worry her. Sometimes if I was going down to visit her with a friend I would call first to give her some warning so she could tidy up if she needed to, but she never bothered. More times than not it would be Andrew going round with the duster when they were together, while she sat on the sofa watching him. Leaving the house like this wasn't like her.

'What about the keys?' I asked Gary through the window, the feeling of foreboding inside me making my voice croak uncomfortably in my throat.

'Can't find them anywhere,' he said.

Kevin, sensing our worry was starting to cry. 'Where's me mammy?' he wanted to know, in his little toddler voice.

'Pass the phone out to me,' I told Gary, cuddling Kevin at the same time and trying to comfort him. 'I'm calling the police to see if there's been any accidents in the night that she could have been involved in.'

That was the only explanation I could think of, that she had been in a crash in the pizza van and was lying unconscious in a hospital somewhere with no means of identification on her. That would be why she hadn't called to tell me. I got straight through to the station and explained that my daughter had disappeared during the night and asking if they knew of any reported accidents.

'There's been no incidents that we know about,' the duty officer said, 'and it's too soon to report someone missing. I suggest you make the house safe and then go back home and wait for your daughter to phone you from wherever she is.'

I had wanted to hear something more proactive than that, but I could see it was all I was going to get for the moment. To make the house safe we were going to have to do something about the window Gary had broken. I went back to the man across the road and told him what was going on. He said he had some wood and would bring it over. Gary climbed back out through the window and between them they boarded it up. I was feeling so agitated, desperate to do something positive to sort the situation out, that I could hardly stand still. As a mother it didn't feel possible that one of my children could just disappear off the face of the earth without leaving any trace of where she had gone or why; it felt as if I was trapped in a bad dream.

Kath from next door looked out again and I went over to talk to her at her back door, asking her to keep an eye on the house for me. If Julie came back, she was to get her to ring me straight away. I could see her son sitting in the kitchen with one of his friends. She promised to call me immediately if she saw anything at all.

Next I drove down to find Charlie at his catering van, fighting to keep my rising panic under control. He was already open for business, serving customers through the hatch, and he looked surprised to see me parking up and hurrying over.

'Our Julie's missing,' I blurted out the moment I got to the hatch, struggling to keep the tears back, hoping he would be able to calm me down with some logical explanation.

'What do you mean?' He looked totally puzzled as if I was talking a different language.

'I've been to the house and she's not there. I've no idea where she is.'

'I'll close up and come home,' he said, immediately starting to pack up. Seeing him take it so seriously I knew I wasn't overreacting and my worry increased.

Once we were back at home I rang everyone I could think of to ask if they'd seen her. I made the calls as quick as possible, nervous that if I wasn't careful I would be on the phone at the moment Julie tried to ring and I would miss the call. No one I spoke to had any more idea where she could be than I did. After an hour or so I went down to the pizza shop, pressing my face to the glass, my hands cupped over my eyes to try to see if there was any sign of life yet, but the premises were still all closed up and dark inside. Just a few hours before they would have been buzzing with activity and Julie would have been part of it; now the shop was as silent and deserted as her house.

The hours were ticking past. Her appointed time at the court came and went and still there was no call. Now

it didn't seem likely that she had just overslept somewhere, but what other explanation could there be? I did-
n't know what to do with myself. I just wanted to find
her and put my mind at rest. Charlie wasn't saying much
but I could tell he was as puzzled and worried as I was.
We both knew this wasn't like her and when you don't
have any facts to go on, your mind always tends to go
straight to the worst possible explanations. Neither of us
wanted to voice the fears that were beginning to grow
inside us. We wanted to put that moment off for as long
as possible.

In the afternoon we left Kevin with Angela and went
back down to the pizza shop again. This time, to my
relief, the lights were on. We could see people moving
around at the back preparing the ovens and the ingredients for the evening's orders.

'Our Julie's disappeared,' I told them the moment we
were in through the door. 'Which of you took her home
last night?'

We must have been sounding frantic by then, and
maybe they felt we were accusing them of something,
because they seemed to become evasive, all denying they
knew anything, shrugging their shoulders and avoiding
our eyes, which made us even more angry and panicked.
They were talking nervously amongst themselves in
their own language, making us wonder what they were
talking about, making us feel left out and suspicious. We

just wanted a simple answer to the question of who had dropped her off at the house and when. We just wanted them to help us, to give us some clue as to where she might be, what her movements might have been after she finished work the night before. Why would this be causing them such a problem? We couldn't make head or tail of what was going on.

'Why won't you tell me who dropped her off last night? What's your problem?'

I couldn't understand why they weren't being more helpful; every way we turned we seemed to bang into a brick wall. The police weren't willing to accept she was a missing person yet and these people wouldn't tell us what they knew about her movements during the night. The neighbours knew no more than we did and nor did her friends. There was no one else for us to ask. What had happened to Julie? Why were these people acting so suspiciously? It was as if she had been abducted from her bed by aliens and everyone was frightened to tell us the truth.

Gary and Charlie were both getting heated and frustrated by the Iranians' defensiveness and I could see there was going to be a fight, so I went out onto the pavement to get out of the way and leave them all to it. There was some angry shouting going on behind me and one of the Iranians came out of the kitchen brandishing a knife sharpener, wanting to chase Charlie and Gary out of the shop. He lunged at them and there were some blows exchanged. Someone must have called the police because the next thing I knew there was a patrol car tearing round the corner and screeching to a halt outside the shop.

I tried to explain the situation, but the Iranians complained that Charlie and Gary had attacked them. After some more shouting and gesticulating, they were carted off to the police station leaving me in shock on the pavement outside.

The Iranians went back to preparing their pizzas, talking angrily amongst themselves. Everything had become a thousand times worse and I was frantic now. I needed Charlie and Gary to help me look for Julie and the police wouldn't tell me what was going on or whether they were going to be charging them with anything. No one seemed to want to tell us anything. The whole world was going mad around us.

Charlie and Gary were kept in the cells overnight. Angela and I spent the evening alone and desperate, trying to keep things normal for Kevin. We couldn't understand why our whole world had suddenly been turned upside down, with our family vanishing all around us. Every hour of that night felt like an eternity. I was beginning to wonder if I would ever sleep peacefully again.

Friday dawned and nothing had changed. Julie was still gone. We hadn't heard from her since Wednesday.

The police let Charlie and Gary go and when they got home Charlie told me he had hardly slept during the night because it had been so cold and they hadn't given him a blanket. They wouldn't even let him stop off at home on the way to the station to get some blood-pressure tablets that he needed to take every day. One of the policemen on duty had accused him of being bad-tempered when in fact he was just frantic with worry about Julie and where she might be. It was all adding to my feeling that the entire world had turned against us and wanted to obstruct our search for Julie in any way they could.

Charlie and Gary were sent home without any apology or explanation. We actually had to ask the police later what was going to happen and it was only then that they told us charges against them had been dropped. I probably would have had a lot more to say about the matter if I hadn't been so beside myself with worry about Julie. I was desperate to get the police to help us and I didn't want to alienate them if I could help it.

Eventually, once they realized they weren't in any sort of trouble, one of the Iranians admitted that he had dropped Julie home at about one-thirty in the morning, and that he had seen her put her key in the door before he had driven away. At last we had a piece of the jigsaw, which we could use to start building a picture of what might have happened during the night. We now knew she had gone home and she had gone into the house. The chances that she would then have gone out again at that time of night to visit anyone else seemed small. But the information still didn't make the overall picture any clearer; if anything it made it even more confusing. If she had been in the house at one-thirty, how could she just have been spirited away between then and seven-thirty?

The feeling of foreboding in my stomach was a hundred times worse than it had been the day before. It seemed as though I had exhausted every possibility of places to go looking for her. Something had definitely gone very badly wrong. It was time to insist that the police became involved in the search, whether they wanted to or not. The police view was that Julie had not been missing long enough to cause concern, but I didn't care about that. Julie had vanished from behind the closed curtains of her own house and we needed them to go looking for her. We drove to Billingham police station and found a woman sergeant on the desk as we walked in.

'Our daughter's disappeared,' I told her, fighting to hold myself together.

'Disappeared?' she asked, one eyebrow arched sceptically, her jaw methodically chewing on a piece of gum.

'Yes,' I said. 'I want to report her missing.'

'When did she go missing?'

'I last saw her the day before yesterday, in the afternoon.'

'It's too soon to report her missing,' she said, still chewing, acting as if this sort of thing happened all the time. 'There's probably a logical explanation.'

'Like what?' I asked.

'She probably came home from work and decided to go to a nightclub.' She shrugged. 'Maybe she got drunk and she's sleeping it off somewhere.'

'For a day and a half? She wouldn't do that,' I protested. 'She's got a young child. She was due to appear in court yesterday morning.'

'Listen,' Charlie interrupted and I could hear from the gruffness of his voice that he was getting annoyed again. 'Our daughter's disappeared mysteriously and we want to know what's happened to her. If you won't take our statement we'll go to the main police station in Stockton.'

Other officers were appearing from behind the scenes to help the desk sergeant with what must by then have seemed like a pair of difficult customers. They must have realized we weren't going to just go away and so they decided to pacify us, promising they would send someone round to take a statement from us the next morning.

We hardly slept at all on the Friday night either, waiting for the phone to ring and to hear Julie's voice giving us some logical explanation about where she'd been. My mind was whirring over all the terrible possibilities, picturing unimaginable scenes as the hours ticked past. She had never left it this long between phone calls home, never gone a whole day without speaking to us in her whole life. I knew for sure that something really bad must have happened. Someone must have taken her and be holding her prisoner, or she was wandering around somewhere with a lost memory, or she was dead. By that second day, I was thinking the worst. I felt totally helpless, half of me wanting to get out and scour every street in the area and the other half not wanting to move from the phone in case she called.

Kevin was crying most of the time, wanting to know where his mammy was, sensing the tension amongst the grown-ups. We were finding it really hard to come up with cheerful answers to his questions or to think of anything to say that might placate him. Distracting a small child when you are already distracted yourself is an almost impossible task, but we all did our best.

We rang Andrew's mum and dad and asked them to get in touch with Andrew down in London because we didn't have a contact number for him. There was just a chance Julie could have turned up there, although I couldn't think for a second why she would do that on the day when she was meant to be going to court to become legally separated from him. Perhaps she had changed her mind about the whole separation thing; but if that was the case, why hadn't she rung to tell me?

They rang back after speaking to him to tell us Andrew knew no more about where Julie could be than we did. It didn't surprise me but it meant one more avenue of hope had been closed off.

The next morning, Saturday, a policeman and woman arrived at the house to take our statements. The young man, PC Newman, may have thought he was trying to put our minds at rest but to us it seemed that he was being totally unsympathetic and offhand in the way he talked to us.

'She's a perfect case of someone who would be likely to just take off,' he said.

'What do you mean?' I asked, my hackles rising at being told about my own daughter by a complete stranger.

'I've been in community relations for several years,' he said, as if he knew everything about everything. 'She's a typical case; she had marriage problems; she was due to go to court. She's probably come in from work to a cold, dark, empty house and decided to make a fresh start. Knowing the boy was safely looked after by you, she's probably walked down to the A19 and hitched a ride to London.'

'You must be joking,' Charlie exploded. 'It's totally out of character.'

'Listen,' I chipped in, 'you're dealing with a stranger, and I'm dealing with a daughter and I'm telling you as a mother that she has not just taken off to London. Something has happened to her, I know it has. I can feel it in my gut.'

I could see that no matter what we said he was never going to believe us. He just thought we were hysterical parents while he was the professional and must therefore know better. It was becoming obvious to us the police weren't going to do anything, not until Julie had been gone at least a few days. But how could we sit around for even a moment longer without doing anything? Suppose she was trapped somewhere and needed our help? How could we stop ourselves from going mad without knowing what was going on? How were we going to be able to bear it if we weren't actively doing something about the situation? Everything that was happening to us was the opposite of any parental instincts we might have; it was pure torture.

I considered the idea that she might have gone to London. Apart from Andrew, she only knew one person there – an old school friend called Margaret who worked with Down's Syndrome kids. Julie had visited her the year before, the only time I can remember her travelling anywhere on her own. It had been a big adventure for her, which was one of the reasons why I had known she would never just disappear off to

London without saying anything. I didn't have a contact number for Margaret but I told the police about her and they tracked her down. She rang me after that to say she hadn't heard anything from Julie.

On Sunday, after another sleepless night, our brains stretched to breaking point by a mixture of worry and exhaustion, we went back down to Grange Avenue to see if any of the neighbours had managed to remember anything at all that might shed some light on what had happened.

When you have no idea what is going on you tend to grasp any straw that is offered to you, however flimsy it might be. When Kath from the house next door said that a police friend of her son Mark had rung him to say they'd had an anonymous tip-off, we immediately took it seriously. The tip-off had come to the police from a woman caller who had told them she had seen a drunk woman being bundled into a car by three men behind the pizza shop in the middle of the night that Julie had disappeared. The image filled me with fear, but at least it gave a possible clue that the police might be able to follow up. When I rang them to ask about it, they were shocked that I knew anything about it at all.

'That information should be confidential,' I was told. 'It was an anonymous call.'

In the end the lead came to nothing as no one else ever came forward to back up the story and the anonymous caller never rang back, so I was left feeling angry with the police yet again, feeling they had acted unprofessionally by gossiping about Julie with the neighbours when they had nothing to follow up with.

Despite this set-back we still talked and talked to anyone who would give us the time, but no one knew anything else. Every way we turned we were faced with more brick walls, not given even a single lead to follow.

Later on that Sunday, I drove down to Stockton police station, determined to keep on pestering them until I found someone who would take us seriously, who would believe that what we were saying was true and that it was impossible to think that Julie had just run off to London. I didn't expect them to greet me with open arms, but I was past caring what sort of reactions I got by then. They could think I was the most hysterical and annoying woman in the world for all I cared, as long as they did something about looking for Julie. There's a saying that it's the wheel that squeaks the loudest that gets the oil first. I intended to keep on making as loud a noise as I could till they did something that would shut me up.

There was a long queue at the counter when I walked into the police station and my stomach was churning with the tension by the time I came to the front. My brain was fuddled with a mixture of anxiety

and exhaustion, so when I looked up and saw the Iranians from the 'Mr Macaroni' pizza shop being led down
the stairs, something snapped in my head. I started
screaming hysterically at them: 'What have you done
with my daughter?'

Seeing them there, I assumed they must have been
brought in for questioning, that they must be suspected
of something. They had behaved strangely when we
went to see them and now the police had brought them
in. I jumped straight to the worst conclusions and probably would have attacked them physically if there hadn't
been police around to hold me back. The sergeant who
had been handling the desk quickly steered me away
from everyone else and took me to a side office where he
introduced me to a detective called Inspector Geoff Lee.
They invited me to sit and tried to calm me down. I certainly had their attention now, even if it was only because
they thought I was an hysterical mad woman who was
likely to attack innocent people in their station.

'I'm telling you as a mother,' I ranted on, 'something
has happened to my daughter. This is totally out of character for her; she wouldn't disappear off to London. She
wouldn't even go into town on her own; she always liked
company wherever she went. This is a girl I see every
day; go and check with other people; ask the neighbours,
they'll tell you she's always round at my house. Everyone
knows that.'

'We are taking you seriously,' Inspector Lee assured me. 'We are making enquiries. We're going to send a team of forensic officers into the house tomorrow.'

Part of me was relieved that they were finally listening to me and believing that I might be right, but another part of me felt a terrible foreboding at the thought of what they might find once they started searching. I wanted them to take me seriously and believe me, but I didn't want to be proved right. I would have given anything to get a call from Julie now to say she was down in London. I don't doubt I would have given her an earful for all the worry she had caused us, but how wonderful it would have felt to be able to do that. Supposing I was never going to be able to talk to her again? The thought was unbearable.

I kept going over and over the same things in my mind. If the police were willing to send in a forensics team then they must think there was a chance I was right and that something terrible had happened to Julie. I wasn't sure how I would be able to cope with finally finding out the truth, but I also knew I couldn't go on much longer not knowing anything.

Chapter Six

The Search

The following morning, Monday 20 November, five forensic officers went into the little three-bedroom house in Grange Avenue. Five men, I thought, should be more than enough to comb every inch of the place from top to bottom in search of evidence; after all, how many potential hiding places for clues could there be in such a small house? At last someone was doing something positive and it felt as if we might actually be moving towards discovering some answers to all the questions we had been endlessly asking ourselves over the previous few days.

If anything had happened to Julie in that house during the previous Wednesday night they would now discover what it was, using all their scientific knowledge and policing experience. I'd seen lots of crime programmes on television, both documentaries and dramas, and it seemed that forensic teams pretty much always got their man. Part of me was terrified to even think what they would find, while the other part was relieved that people in authority finally believed me and were taking my fears seriously. These were people who would know what to do next, once they had established the facts; at least, that was what I told myself.

To have five highly trained forensic experts combing the house seemed encouraging, although it was hard to imagine why it needed quite so many men for such a limited space. We were pleased they were being so thorough, but worried that they must be expecting to find something bad. With all their clever tests and progress with DNA matching I was confident we would soon find out where Julie was. In bad moments I felt sure she had been killed and we would soon be finding her body, but in moments of hope I thought perhaps they would work out where she had disappeared to and we would all be reunited soon. You have to have those tiny slices of hope just to keep you going from day to day, however irrational they may be. They are the things that stop you from tipping over into complete madness.

Every minute of each day we seemed to be waiting for something to happen; waiting for Julie to ring or for the police to call and tell us they had found something in the house. When you are waiting without knowing what you are waiting for, every hour seems to last forever. Most of the time is filled with talking over and over the same things, asking one another the same questions over endless cups of tea.

I suppose I had thought they would come up with something almost the moment they crossed the threshold, but there was only a terrible silence from the house as they continued to go about their business behind closed doors and police cordons. I kept picturing all those men going through Julie's personal belongings, picking her life into minute pieces, finding out everything about her and making judgements about what sort of girl she was. It felt as though our family had been invaded.

Every time the phone went, we would snatch it up before it had even had time to ring twice but it was always a well-meaning friend or relative wanting to know if there was any news. We had nothing to tell them because the police said nothing. On the Wednesday, a week after I last saw Julie, Inspector Lee finally rang.

'Will you and your younger daughter go down to the house,' he asked, 'to see if any of Julie's clothing is missing? We'll send a policewoman to fetch you.'

Of course we agreed instantly, glad to have something positive that we could do, but both Angela and I were nervous at the thought of being in the house with so many policemen, to be walking around a potential

crime scene. What if one of us said the wrong thing?
What if we weren't able to help them?

We waited for the policewoman to come for us but the
hours kept going past and we were becoming more and
more worried. Eventually I rang Julie's number to speak
to the police in the house, hoping to find out what was
going on. One of the forensic team picked up the phone.

'It's Julie's mum here,' I said. 'The policewoman has-
n't come for us.'

'She should be there in about half an hour,' he promised.

'Have you found anything?' I asked, unable to contain my curiosity for a second longer.

'There's no dead bodies in here,' he replied, 'if that's
what you mean.'

I felt as though I'd been punched in the stomach. He
had spoken out loud the words that had been circling
round and round in my head ever since Gary first broke
into the house and found it silent and deserted. The
words I hadn't dared to speak out loud.

'Do you think I needed to hear that?' I snapped. 'I
know my daughter's dead and I don't need you to tell
me.'

I slammed the phone down, furious at his insensitiv-
ity and shocked to hear my own words. I felt dizzy. It
was the first time I had actually voiced the fear that I had
been thinking about almost from the start. Boiling with

fury at the man's tactlessness, I rang Inspector Lee and told him what the detective had just said to me.

'Leave it with me,' he said, obviously aware of just how upset I was becoming. 'The policewoman will be with you very shortly.'

When the policewoman arrived and took us down to the house the detective I'd spoken to was waiting outside for us.

'Mrs Ming,' he said, 'I just wanted to apologize for what I said. I didn't mean to upset you.'

I let him know exactly what I thought of him, which he took manfully, and then let them lead us into the house. I was in a daze, trying to be as helpful as possible but finding it hard to keep my emotions in check. I could remember that on the last afternoon I'd seen her, Julie had been wearing a black skirt and a peach-coloured blouse. They were the only clothes that Angela and I couldn't find as we searched through the wardrobe. I told the police.

'I don't see any shoes missing either,' I added. 'If she'd gone down to London she would have taken shoes, wouldn't she?'

The policeman nodded his acceptance of what I was saying but said nothing himself. We went through into the bathroom and looked around.

'Look at this,' I told them, pointing to a bag on the side. 'Are you suggesting she has taken off to London and left her make-up bag? Our Julie wouldn't go down the road without putting her make-up on, let alone a big city. She wouldn't even have stepped outside the house.'

I could see from the way the head of the forensic team was looking at me that he thought I was a neurotic mother; that I was too emotionally involved to be thinking clearly. But I knew that however untidy Julie might have kept the house, she was always neat with her own appearance. Her hair was always elaborately done and her make-up perfectly applied. There was no way she would have walked out without taking these things with her; someone else must have forced her out of the house against her will, or worse.

By the time we left Grange Avenue I was shaking, even more certain that something terrible had happened to Julie, and feeling not a single inch closer to knowing what it might be. I couldn't understand how the police could have been in there for three whole days already and not come up with anything.

Time continued to drag past and on the Friday, when their investigations were finally complete, Inspector Lee came to see us to tell us the result of their five days' work. It was hard to imagine how so many men could have managed to spend that long searching such a small house.

'I can't guarantee you that your daughter hasn't come to grief somewhere in the country,' he said as we all sat awkwardly round our front room. 'But I *can* guarantee you that nothing untoward happened to her inside that house.'

In other words they had found nothing. Not a single clue. They were still as mystified as Gary and I had been when we first discovered the neat, empty house. Julie might as well have been abducted by aliens for all they could tell us. I jumped out of my chair, too agitated to sit still a moment longer.

'If you are certain that nothing happened to her in that house,' I said, 'then I'm telling you she can't have been in there. But I know something has happened to her, and we are pretty sure she went into that house after being dropped off.'

Inspector Lee just stared at me as if I was daft, unable to think of anything to say that would calm me down or satisfy me. As far as he was concerned his team had done their best. They had listened to me and acted on what I had told them, but I had been proved wrong. I couldn't understand it. None of it made sense. I had been so sure that the forensic team would have uncovered at least some evidence that would lead us to an explanation of what had gone on. Perhaps Inspector Lee thought the fact that they had found nothing would help to put my mind at rest, but it actually did the opposite because it raised even more new questions without answering any of the existing ones. It didn't seem possible, or bearable, that we were still no further on and yet the investigation was over. But it was true. Yet another long weekend of fear now stretched ahead of us, and who knew how much longer after that?

The police believed they had done all they could for the moment. They had responded to my request for help and they had found nothing. Maybe they felt they had been vindicated, that they had been right all along in believing that Julie had run off to start a new life, and I was just a silly, hysterical mother who didn't know when to let go of her children.

Their work done, the house in Grange Avenue was locked up again, as dark and silent and empty as it had been on the morning when I first went round to find her. Because Julie's keys were still missing the police had changed the lock on the back door so they could get in and out while they were investigating.

'We've also put an alarm in the house,' Inspector Lee explained, 'which doesn't sound on the premises but will ring in the police station if anyone tries to get in with Julie's keys.'

The following morning, he called to tell us that the house had been broken into during the night. The alarm had malfunctioned, he said, and the intruder had got away with the video.

'How did they get in?' Charlie wanted to know.

'Through one of the front windows,' he said.

Once the police were off the phone we drove down to have a look but there was no sign of forced entry on any of the windows. Charlie phoned the inspector back and told him that we couldn't understand what it was they were saying had happened.

'Did you look in the loft properly while you were there?' Charlie asked while he was on the phone. It was something that had been worrying us, since we couldn't think of anywhere else in the house where anything could be hidden.

'Do you think we're thirteen-year-old school kids?' the inspector retorted angrily. 'We're professional police officers.'

We knew we were getting on their nerves with our continual questions and our refusal to accept what they were certain was the truth – that Julie had just walked out of our lives without saying anything. But we were her parents and we were so frantic with worry we wanted to check every possible thing that might have happened to our daughter. They might have a hundred other cases to be getting on with but we had nothing else to think about apart from what had happened to Julie. They could put her file to one side, telling themselves they had done all they could, but we couldn't do that with the terrible unhappiness and uncertainty that filled our heads and made our hearts feel like lead.

Every day was another nightmare, with Kevin continually asking us where his mammy was and us not able to think of anything convincing to say. We just kept telling him that we were sure she wouldn't be away for long, having no idea at what stage we would have to tell him something different. How could we tell him that his mammy might be dead if there was still even a remote possibility that she could walk back through the door?

He must have overheard things that made him worry. There were too many people coming and going around him for him not to be aware that something was badly wrong, that his family were all deeply unhappy. At the same time, having him around was probably the only thing that kept us sane, because we had to hold ourselves together at least a little in order to be able to look after him. Andrew came back from London to help look after Kevin, but none of us were going near the house in Grange Avenue. We didn't have keys for the new locks anyway. As far as we knew the alarm to the police station was still in there and had been mended, and we would be informed if anyone came back to the house, either an intruder or Julie herself.

Although they now knew better than to keep saying it to me, the police obviously still favoured the idea that she had gone down to London, and I certainly wanted that to be true. I wanted the feeling in my guts to be wrong. I wanted more than anything for the police to be proved right, even though there had been no sightings of her or any other glimmers of hope. Would she really have gone without telling a single living soul, when she had never before been known to go anywhere without ringing us a hundred times to tell us about it, or to ask me to go with her?

The police were treating it as a normal missing persons case, and they asked us to do an appeal in the local paper. We were happy to go along with it, to feel that we might just be talking directly to Julie, that she might be alive somewhere and she might respond to our pleas. But if we were only talking to the local paper, was she likely to see it if she was down in London, as they kept suggesting? They assured us this would be the best thing to do; I suppose it was their standard procedure in such cases.

Our solicitor, with whom we were spending a lot of time by then, suggested we go on Tyne Tees Television as well, to try to reach her that way. We were happy to agree, even though talking to the cameras with Kevin on my knee made it impossible for me to hold back the tears. We were willing to try anything. If Julie was alive we just wanted her to let us know she was okay, we wanted her to know that we all loved her and that we were desperate with worry. I was sure if she realized that, then she would also realize she had to make contact to put our minds at rest. If she saw Kevin's little face she wouldn't be able to stay away from him another day.

As long as the police hadn't found a body we still had some hope, and however faint it might be it was just enough to keep us going from one agonizing day to the next, from one hour to the next. Making the appeals gave us something to think about, something to distract us from the pain of the anxiety and fear knotting our stomachs and weighing down our hearts. I needed to be busy and distracted every moment of the day because if I wasn't the thoughts would start to crowd in and I wouldn't know how I was going to be able to keep going.

Christmas was approaching and every happy, smiling face or cheerful Christmas carol was a reminder of just how empty and fearful our lives had become. We wrapped presents for Julie and put them under the tree, all ready for her to return, and we did yet another appeal in the newspaper.

Inspector Lee was in touch with us most days and he tried to find positive things to say to keep us going. His attitude was that 'no news was good news'. As long as we didn't find a body, he said, there was still a chance that Julie was alive somewhere, although none of us could think of any plausible explanation why she might have chosen that moment to vanish.

'Julie's description is in the main police computer now,' he explained, 'so if anything is found anywhere in the country it will be traced back to Stockton.'

'Why don't you do a national appeal if you're so sure she's in London?' I wanted to know.

'No, we don't need to do that,' he insisted. 'We'll keep it local.'

Did that mean they didn't really believe she was in London any more than I did? Were they just saying they did in order to give me some hope? It was announced in the local papers that they were sending out divers to search the pond and dogs onto the wastelands surrounding Billingham, but were they just going through the motions to humour us? Were they simply biding their time until a body showed up somewhere, which would provide us with all the answers we needed? There was no way of telling.

It was my birthday on 22 December and Inspector Lee told us that if there was one day that Julie was most likely to get in touch, that would be it. He suggested we warn all our friends and family not to ring, so that the line would be clear all day and there was no chance she would fail to get through. It was another hope for us to cling to. All day we sat beside the phone, never moving from the house for fear of missing the call, hardly daring even to go to the bathroom. Every minute was an agonizing silence as we stared at the silent instrument, desperately willing it to ring. By ten o'clock that night we knew she wasn't going to call. If she didn't phone me on my birthday, what hope was there that she would do it any other day?

Inspector Lee called the next day to see if there was any good news, but we had nothing to tell him. Although he hadn't been able to find our Julie for us, he had always shown a personal interest, as if he really cared about what we were going through and wanted to lessen our pain in any way he could. We appreciated that.

'Maybe she'll phone over Christmas,' he said, desperately trying to find something encouraging to say. But she didn't and we had to sit there watching the rest of the world enjoying their holiday while we waited, staring at Julie's unopened presents.

Nor did she call to wish us a happy new year. On New Year's Eve I was watching the crowds in Trafalgar Square on the television, staring hard at all the happy, smiling faces, wondering if Julie was anywhere amongst them, lost to us in the streets of London. The size of the crowds made me despair. If she had chosen to disappear, there was no chance we would ever find her amongst that lot.

Once the first of January had passed Inspector Lee had no new suggestions to make to keep our spirits up, and the future stretched ahead of us like a huge empty canvas, devoid of hope.

January dragged past, cold and grey and miserable, with none of us knowing if we would ever see Julie again. I would stare out the window at the frost and pray that her body wasn't lying out there somewhere, cold and alone. She never liked being on her own. If she was dead I hoped she hadn't suffered, that she had been allowed to die with some dignity.

Frustrated with the lack of effort from the police to go national with their appeals, I contacted the *People* newspaper, because they run a book of missing people. They told me there was a queue of families waiting to get their loved ones onto the list and they would let me know when Julie's details reached the front of the queue. The thought that there were so many missing people all over the country just made it all seem even more hopeless. How could we expect the police to keep dedicating time to the search for Julie if she was just one more statistic amongst thousands? For each of the names on the list there was a family somewhere, just like us, going out of their minds with worry, unable to get on with their own lives until they found out what had happened to their loved one.

Even though I often felt sure in my heart that Julie was dead, I couldn't quite bring myself to extinguish the last flicker of hope, because once that was gone what would I be left with? We had to keep on going for Julie, for Kevin and for our own sanity.

Chapter Seven

Finding Julie

At the end of January the police said there was no more they could do at Grange Avenue and they gave Andrew the keys to the new locks they had installed. He had been staying at a friend's house ever since coming back from London and Kevin had been sleeping with us at night, seeing his dad during the days if Andrew wasn't working. Now they needed a place to live, so Andrew decided he would move back in to Grange Avenue with Kevin and try to rebuild their lives together from there. Charlie and I were both grateful to think that our grandson had a good father who loved him and was going to look after him whether Julie came back or not.

In the moments when I chose to believe that Julie was still alive, I felt sad to think that my daughter might have walked out on her little son. We had always brought the children up to believe family members should look after one another and I was disappointed to think that she might have let us all down so badly. But it just seemed such an impossible thing to believe about her that my head would start spinning again.

I went down to the house with Andrew to collect and take away all Julie's clothes. If Kevin was going to be living there I didn't want him coming across his mam's possessions, making him wonder and ask more questions about where she was and why she had left us. It was important that he just got used to life without her, just in case she never came back. He needed to be helped to forget about her until he was old enough to handle her memory.

It had been shut up for nearly three months of the winter so the house was freezing cold as we stepped into it, and messy. It seemed sad and desolate; a place that had been left neglected and unloved for too long, making me shiver from more than just the cold. At least, I told myself, we knew that nothing bad had happened to Julie there, because the police had told us so. I wouldn't have wanted Kevin to go back to live there if I thought something had happened to his mam on the premises. I wouldn't want there to be ghosts haunting his young life. Andrew and I packed up all Julie's stuff and I took it back home to sort out.

The first day of February Andrew went back to Grange Avenue again to start clearing up. The police had left a lot of mess with all the fingerprint dust and it was going to take him several days to clean it enough for him and Kevin to move in properly. The first thing he did was switch on the gas heating behind the sitting room fire to try to get rid of the chill and make the place feel more lived in. The radiators creaked and cracked into life and warmth slowly spread through the rooms, forcing out the chill.

He phoned me up at teatime to let me know how he was getting on.

'There's a horrible smell in the bathroom,' he told me.

'That'll be the toilet after all these weeks,' I said. 'Put some bleach down and don't use it for a while.'

That day the *People* rang to say Julie's details would be in the paper on the following Sunday. It was a small shred of hope, but I clung to it anyway. Maybe this time she would see it and would know we were trying to get in touch, or perhaps someone who knew her in her new life would spot it and ring to let us know where she was, realizing that it would put our minds at rest. If she was wandering around somewhere with a lost memory, perhaps someone would recognize her and bring her home. All these remote possibilities were constantly flitting in and out of my mind.

Andrew had told me he wasn't going to go back into the house over the weekend but would be there on the Monday morning to finish the clearing up.

When I woke on the Sunday morning I noticed I had some scratches on the back on my hand. It reminded me of Julie and the way she used to threaten to scratch her brother and sister when they annoyed her. She always kept her nails long. I showed Angela while we were having breakfast.

'This reminds me of Julie,' I told her. 'Maybe she's trying to communicate with us from the other side.'

'Oh, shut up, our Mam,' Angela said, shuddering. 'Stop being so spooky.'

I knew I was probably being silly but I just had a funny feeling, which I couldn't explain. I didn't say any more. That afternoon I was in the car on my own and I started talking out loud to Julie, just as I would have done if she'd been sat beside me.

'If I only knew whether you were dead or alive,' I told her. 'Only I can't carry on any longer like this, not knowing.'

I felt close to my breaking point, as if I soon wouldn't be able to cope even on a day-to-day basis – not even for Kevin's sake.

On the following day I knew Andrew would be back working at the house. I was due to take Kevin to his playgroup at one-thirty so I thought we would drop in on the way to see how Andrew was getting on, and to remind him to pick Kevin up again at three o'clock. We drove down and parked. Kevin wanted to come in to see his dad too so we walked up the front path together. I knocked on the front door and Andrew opened it to us.

'Have you got rid of that smell?' I asked as we went through into the kitchen.

'No,' he said, 'it's getting worse.'

'Oh, get out of the way,' I said. 'I'll go and see for myself.'

I left Kevin chatting happily with his dad in the kitchen and marched upstairs to investigate, wondering why men are always so useless at these sorts of practical things. Halfway up the stairs the stench reached my nostrils. I'd been working for twenty years in an operating theatre by then and deep inside I knew what it was. But my brain wouldn't let me accept that it was possible. There must be some other explanation – a dirty sanitary towel maybe, wedged in a corner somewhere and rotting away. Whatever it was, please God it wasn't Julie.

It was as if I was outside my own body, seeing myself going up those stairs and into the bathroom as if I was watching a CCTV screen. I'm told it's called 'psychic numbing', a condition caused by intense shock. There couldn't be anything that bad in the house, I was telling myself, because the police hadn't found anything. Five forensic officers had been there for five days and had found nothing. Inspector Lee had guaranteed me nothing had happened to Julie inside those walls. 'There's no dead bodies here, if that's what you mean,' the detective had said. There had to be a much simpler explanation for the smell.

As I went into the bathroom it all looked just the same as it had the day I'd been in there with Angela and the police. I looked behind the toilet and behind the basin, but there was nothing hidden there that could have been causing the problem. Before going to London, Andrew had stripped off the wall tiles, intending to replace them, but hadn't yet got round to doing it. I wondered if it might be the fixative on the walls that was making the smell. Please God, let that be what it was.

I leant across the bath to sniff, my knees pressing against the flimsy hardboard panel on the side. The wall smelled of nothing, but the panel was loose and a gap sprang open under the pressure from my leg. The smell suddenly grew much stronger, almost overwhelming.

Whatever was causing the smell was under the bath. Part of my brain told me that I was going to find Julie there, but how was that possible? The police had been in there for a whole five days. They would obviously have found the body if it was there. I was being stupid and melodramatic to even consider such a possibility. So what was it? Maybe a rat had died in there. I had to look and see, to put my mind at rest. I was too confused and it was all happening too fast for me to be able to imagine what effect it would have on me if I did find Julie under there. So many thoughts and feelings were crowding in at once, making it impossible for me to think straight. Working on automatic pilot I knelt down and pulled at the panel so that I could peer behind it.

Even though it was wrapped in a blanket I knew that what I was seeing was a body. The stench billowed out, filling my lungs and making me retch. I let go of the panel, allowing it to spring back into place, and scrambled to get back onto my feet and out of the room, stumbling down the stairs, screaming hysterically for Andrew, the smell filling my lungs and my head, unable to control myself, not even enough to protect Kevin.

'She's under the bath!' I screamed as I half ran and half fell into the kitchen. 'She's under the bath!'

Andrew stared at me blank faced. Later he told me that at that moment he thought I had cracked up. He thought I must have imagined it, my mind finally caving in under the pressure of the previous three months. How could she be there after all this time? After so many police had been in there? After he had spent the last few days working around the house? It didn't seem possible, but I knew what I had seen and what I had smelled and I couldn't get a grip on myself. I too thought I might be about to lose my mind.

Kevin was standing beside me, open-mouthed, staring up at the horror of his hysterical grandmother. I grabbed Andrew's arm.

'Please, tell me it isn't her,' I begged. 'Please.'

'I'll get a screwdriver,' he said, as calmly as he could, 'and take the panel off; see what's there.'

I couldn't stop weeping and shaking, even though poor little Kevin started crying as his dad went upstairs. I lifted him up, hugging him tight, trying to comfort him even though I couldn't even quieten my own sobbing. There were a terrible few seconds of nothing as Andrew must have been undoing the screws, a few moments when it was still possible I had imagined it and that none of it was true, but then I heard his shout as he lifted the panel off and I knew it was all too real.

'Oh, Jesus Christ, no!' he exclaimed.

'What do I do?' he shouted as he thundered down the stairs. 'What do I do?'

'Dial 999!' I yelled.

I put Kevin down and ran out of the house, desperate to get away, frantic to get help. I just wanted it all not to be true. I couldn't think straight, couldn't work out what to do. I was still screaming like a mad woman as I burst into Kath's house next door.

'She's under the bath!' I shrieked. 'She's under the bath!'

I just wanted someone to make the nightmare end, but part of me must have known that no one could do that, and the thought of having to face the truth was too much to bear. How could life possibly go on after this?

How could I go on living with those few moments imprinted on my memory forever?

'She can't be,' Kath shouted back, trying to shock me out my hysterical state. 'She can't be! You've got it wrong. It must be something else. The police have been in.'

'No, I've just seen her,' I insisted. 'She's there.'

Within minutes the street was full of police cars and vans, wailing sirens, shouting voices and hurrying feet. I ran back out, like everyone else in the street. They were all trying to work out what was going on. I saw Inspector Lee getting out of one of the cars and I charged straight at him. I moved so fast none of the others had time to stop me and I grabbed him and pinned him against the fence, punching him and screaming at him. He was the one person in the police force we had been able to relate to during the whole of the previous three months of hell, and I now felt that he had let us down as well. He had promised me she wasn't in there! He had promised!

'I told you she wouldn't have taken off to London but you wouldn't listen,' I screamed.

'We don't know what you've found yet,' he said, attempting to hold me back and retain at least some of his dignity.

'Come on then,' I shouted, challenging him, trying to drag him back into the house and force him to face what Andrew and I had had to face. 'Come and see!'

This was the man who had sworn to me that nothing had happened to Julie in Grange Avenue. He had absolutely guaranteed it. He was the man I had trusted. By the time I got back to the door the police had already taken over, cordoning the house off with their blue striped tape, and they wouldn't let me back in again. There was total confusion everywhere; so many people, so many uniforms. I was still hysterical as they led me away, gently putting me into my car with poor little Kevin, who was crying his eyes out. He didn't know what was wrong, but all the adults being so upset must have been very frightening for him. A policewoman was told to drive us home.

I knew I had to get Kevin away from the house, but part of me didn't want to leave Julie behind. That was my baby back there. I felt I should have been with her, not handing her over to the care of strangers, strangers who had done nothing up till now but let her down, leaving her lying in there like that, all on her own. At the same time I didn't think I could bear to see her again in the state she was in now. And I knew it didn't matter where I went because I was never going to be able to escape the pictures imprinted in my head and the smell in my nostrils. At least Julie had escaped to the other side; I was still trapped here in a hell that was getting worse with every passing moment.

The police went to fetch Charlie and Angela and brought them both home so that we could all be together.

Two policemen were sent to Gary's home in Middlesbrough. When he opened the door to their knock they greeted him with the words, 'We've found your sister.'

'Where was she?' he asked. 'In London?'

'No,' they said, 'under the bath.'

It wasn't until he arrived at our house with the police that he discovered it had actually been me who had found Julie, not them. It seemed as though they were embarrassed to admit what had actually happened, as if they were hoping to gloss over the details about how their search of the house had failed and to give the impression that they had found her with their skilful police work.

There were so many people coming and going from our house in the following hours, so much confusion, that I didn't even notice Andrew had gone missing. Only later did we discover that the police had taken him straight in for questioning. Never for a moment, not even a single second, did it occur to any of us in the family that he could have had anything to do with Julie's death, but I can understand why he might have been at the top of their suspect list. Most murders are committed by close relatives and people that the victim knows. The police knew his relationship with Julie had been going wrong, so obviously he was the first person they would question.

When Inspector Lee arrived at our house later with another policeman I still wasn't able to control my rage towards him for what he had allowed us to go through, and for the way the police had treated us all, and for letting Julie down. Before anyone could stop me I had run at him again, knocking him off his feet and pinning him over the chest freezer in the kitchen, punching him and screaming at him with renewed strength. In the end Charlie had to drag me off before I did him some serious injury. I was so angry I wanted someone else to feel a tiny bit of the pain that I was going through. I wanted someone else to suffer for what I now knew Julie must have suffered. I couldn't imagine how the pain I was feeling at that moment would ever go away. I couldn't imagine how I was going to be able to face the coming hours and days and years.

Chapter Eight

The Aftermath

Inspector Lee stayed with us for a while, bravely facing up to my tirades of abuse, but there was little he could do or say in the face of my hysterics and my anger. All he could do was bow his head and accept responsibility for everything that had gone wrong, which he nobly did.

'I don't know how it happened,' he said, 'but there will be an investigation to find out.'

Eventually, when I had quietened down a bit, he made his excuses and left. A few hours later a copy of the local evening paper plopped through the front door onto the mat, fresh from the printing presses. The front page was covered in a story about a skin specialist in Middlesborough who had been murdered but there was a flash at the bottom of the page, which said: 'Detectives have found a body at 27 Grange Avenue.'

I couldn't believe they'd had the nerve to claim in public that it was they who had found the body, as if it was all part of their on-going investigation; as if dogged police work had triumphed in the end. A reporter on the paper, Paul Daniels, had been helping us with all the appeals over the previous three months, so I immediately dialled his number with trembling fingers.

'I just wondered who gave you that information?' I asked as soon as I got through.

'It was the police press office,' he said.

'Well, you can get it retracted,' I snapped. 'Because it was me who found my daughter, not them.'

I slammed the phone down without another word. The anger inside me hadn't abated, in fact it was still building and I needed someone else to vent it on. I snatched the phone up again and called police headquarters, my fingers trembling as I dialled. I got a duty sergeant on the line and told him I wanted to make a complaint in as calm a voice as I could manage. He asked if I wanted to make an appointment.

'I want to see the Chief Constable,' I said.

'I'm afraid you can't do that,' he told me, sounding as if he thought I was mad to even suggest such impertinence.

'Don't tell me what I can and can't do,' I snapped. 'I want to know why I found our daughter's decomposing body instead of your so-called forensic officers.'

It went very quiet at the other end of the line.

'Is that Mrs Ming?' he asked.

'Yes, it is.'

'Can I ring you back?'

He rang back a few minutes later to say an appointment had been made for me with the Deputy Chief Constable for eleven o'clock the following morning. It seemed that now they had a murder enquiry on their hands they were going to be paying a bit more attention to us.

I was in such an hysterical state I hadn't even noticed that Charlie had slipped out of the house until he came back with our doctor, Dr Geoghegan, who gave me an injection to calm me down. Dr Geoghegan had been really supportive all through the months when we had hoped that Julie was just missing. He had known our family a long time and he had been giving me tranquillizers to help me get through the long days and nights of anxiety. I was grateful to Charlie for going for him and to him for coming that day, even if I didn't show it at the time.

The sedative injection didn't seem to make any difference; I couldn't stop smelling Julie's body, as if I was still in the room with it, and I kept seeing the panel coming away from the bath and then her lying behind it, wrapped in a soiled blanket. It was as if I was continually being transported back in time to that one terrible place and moment, trapped on a repeating loop, like a trailer for a real version of some gruesome horror movie.

'Don't hesitate to come for me at any time,' the doctor told Charlie as he left, 'even if it's the middle of the night.'

To my dazed, shocked and now medicated brain, our house seemed to be full of people coming and going, with nothing making much sense. When something so shocking and horrifying happens it is hard to discern between reality and the nightmares that come with sleep. I was constantly asking myself if I really had seen what I thought I saw or if I was going mad. The surge of adrenaline I had experienced at the discovery was still coursing through my veins and there was no way I was going to be sleeping that night, whatever medication the doctor might give me. My thoughts were rushing everywhere at once and I knew I needed to keep myself busy.

I sat up all night that night, writing out a list of complaints I had against the police from the moment we tried to report Julie missing to the moment I found her body. I brought up every single thing that had angered me, from the leaking of anonymous information by a policeman to Kath's son Mark, to the way Charlie was treated when he was arrested at the pizza shop and carted off to the cells for the night without his blood-pressure tablets. Venting my anger against the police gave me something to focus on, something to distract me from the knowledge that Julie really was dead and would never be coming back, and to keep myself from imagining what could have happened to her in the hours before she ended up under the bath. Not yet having a culprit at whom I could aim my hatred and anger, I was left fuming at police incompetence.

If I had dwelled too long on the thought of her lying there on her own in that cold house for three months I would have been tipped over into complete madness. So I just kept writing and writing, staying angry, focusing on what I was going to do next, how I was going to get justice for Julie and for the rest of our family.

When I first left school I did a secretarial course, like so many girls who didn't really know what they wanted to do for a living. I learned shorthand and typing, but the teachers always told us that if we wanted to make a personal impact on someone with a letter we should always write it in longhand. That little nugget of advice had stayed with me throughout the years and so that was what I did. I didn't invest in a computer, or ask anyone else to type things up for me, I just kept scribbling furiously away, pouring my anger and thoughts and feelings through my pen and out onto sheets and sheets of paper. I didn't ask any legal experts to vet anything I wrote either; I didn't want them telling me what I should and

shouldn't say. I wanted everything to come straight from
the heart. If people were upset by what I had to say, then
so much the better. I wanted to rattle a few cages and
wake a few people up. I wanted to shout my grievances
from the rooftops.

All this activity was just to cover up what I really
wanted, of course. What I really wanted was for Julie
not to be dead and for things to be the same as they had
been three months earlier. It's hard to accept that the one
thing you want more than anything is the one thing that
is totally impossible to achieve.

Charlie was also in a state of shock that night and was
finding it increasingly difficult to cope with my hyper-
activity as the reality and irreversibility of what had happened sank in for both of us. He was exhausted and just
wanted to rest for a bit, so Laurence, his brother, said he
would come with me for my appointment with the
police the next day.

'Oh, look,' Laurence said as we drew up outside to
the police station. 'There's a television crew here. I wonder what's going on?'

I looked where he was pointing and saw a Tyne Tees
outside broadcast lorry parked up. It didn't occur to me
for a second that its presence there might have anything
to do with me. If I had known the police were holding a
press conference about Julie's death in that building that
morning I would have marched straight into it and given

them a piece of my mind – and a very good story for their readers and viewers at the same time.

The Deputy Chief Constable, Jack Ord, and another high-ranking officer were waiting for us in the entrance hall, as if we were visiting dignitaries. It was very different to the reception we'd received from the gum-chewing desk sergeant when we'd first come to report Julie missing. He led us courteously into his office.

'May I,' he said once we were settled, 'on behalf of Cleveland Constabulary, offer our condolences?'

'I don't want your condolences,' I snapped, not being in the mood for any of this flannel. I was like a mad woman. 'I want answers to these questions.'

I flung the piece of paper I'd been working on through the night down onto the desk in front of him. The two men glanced quickly at my list of complaints and exchanged worried looks.

'You haven't given us time to put things right, Mrs Ming,' Ord said. 'You're putting in a complaint in less than twenty-four hours.'

'Put things right?' I yelled. 'What the hell are you going to put right?'

He told me that another high-ranking officer from Northumbria Police was on his way to start an investigation into Cleveland Police and their handling of our case. No wonder they were all suddenly being so polite and attentive – they were under investigation themselves.

'I'm going to introduce you to a detective called Sandra in a minute,' he went on, 'who is going to be acting as your liaison officer.'

I was having trouble taking in what was being said to me. I just felt that I had to do something but I had no idea what it was. My daughter had been murdered and I couldn't just sit back and let everyone else take over my family's life, especially given their track record so far. I knew that nothing was going to bring our Julie back, but I had to do whatever I could to find out what had gone wrong. I had to do that for Julie's sake. I couldn't just leave it to a load of bungling police officers to investigate one another, could I? But what choice did I have?

At the end of the meeting Sandra, the liaison officer, followed us back home in her car. Once we got there she came in with us, sat us down and explained that the missing persons team had now been taken off the case and been replaced by the murder squad. As I calmed down Charlie said he thought I should ring Inspector Lee and apologize for the way I'd attacked him the day before. I decided he was right. Inspector Lee had been the one who had been kindest to us throughout the three months; it wasn't really his fault what had happened, even if it was his team that had messed up. But when I tried to ring the station to speak to him they wouldn't put me through, telling me that he was now off the case.

It seemed odd that I couldn't even talk to him on the phone, but I was learning a lot about police procedures. He had gone from being our main point of contact to being completely out of our lives.

That afternoon Andrew rang from Stockton police station asking us to go and pick him up and it was only then that we realized he'd been gone all that time. The police had held him overnight since we found Julie. I don't know where I thought he was during those long hours but there were just too many people around and too many thoughts in my head for me to worry about someone who wasn't there. I suppose I had assumed he was at home with his mum and dad, trying to recover from the shock of what he'd been through in some peace and quiet.

After questioning him for about thirty hours the police had decided that Andrew really didn't know anything more than he was telling them and they let him go. They didn't even offer him a lift home, just showed him the door. The poor man broke down and cried as soon as we had him in the car. He was obviously still in the same state of shock I was in but with the added pressure of having been under intense interrogation for twenty-four hours.

'They told me you were in the next room,' he explained when he could get the words out, 'and that you'd told them I'd phoned you from the house and asked you to come and take the panel off the bath because I thought there was something behind it.'

'There's no way I told them anything like that,' I protested.

'I know. They were just trying to get me to admit I'd put her there and that I wanted you to find her to avert suspicion from myself.'

As if failing to find her body under the bath wasn't bad enough, when the murder squad went up into the loft at Grange Avenue to instigate another search they found Julie's diary, cash card and watch, all casually thrown up there for anyone to see. Yet when Charlie had asked Inspector Lee if he was sure the forensic team had searched the loft thoroughly, the inspector had accused Charlie of treating his officers like thirteen-year-olds. It seemed to us that even thirteen-year-olds would have been able to find those pieces of evidence.

Later we discovered that a total of twenty-nine different police officers had been through that house in the course of those three months, and none of them had spotted any of the clues, let alone the body.

Sandra, our liaison officer, turned out to be a very nice woman, but by the end of the first week of the investigation she was so traumatized by what she was hearing that she burst into tears while she was sitting with us and told me that because of what I'd been through she wasn't able to go into her own bathroom any more.

I ended up comforting her rather than the other way round and she went off sick after only a week. I believe she ended up leaving the police force altogether, unable to take the strain.

Nobody allocated us a new liaison officer initially and even Derrick Dobson, who we were told was the senior investigating officer on the murder squad, didn't bother to make contact with us. We did, however, get to see him talking on the television evening news, calling himself 'the Hunter'.

'I will hunt down this killer,' he assured the viewing public. 'Julie's killer will be found.'

It was as if our own lives were drifting away from us, becoming public property. Other people we knew nothing about had Julie's body now and they had whatever clues and information there might be, while we were left without any idea how to get through each day without her. Often we learned what was happening in our own lives from the television or the newspapers, at the same time as the rest of the world.

The doctor had given me some more tranquillizers and I was trying to cope with looking after Kevin and getting on with our normal lives as best I could, while at the same time following everything that was happening with the police and trying to come to terms with my grief. Charlie, Gary and Angela were crying the whole time but I kept looking for things to do, to keep myself occupied. Amongst other things, I started a scrapbook of press cuttings and pasted in any articles I found about the case.

After a couple of weeks we were assigned a new detective called Mark Braithwaite as our liaison officer. He was a tall, good-looking, very nice man, who was a sergeant at the time and number three on the murder team. He was to become a close friend over the following years, sharing our many trials and tribulations, our hopes and our disappointments. He has since gone on to become a Detective Chief Superintendent and Head of Crime for Cleveland Police and we still talk regularly.

During the coming months our house always seemed to be full of police officers, either local ones from the murder squad or officers from Northumbria who were investigating the Cleveland branch. We also had Kevin there and Andrew had decided he didn't want the boy to be told that his mother had been murdered, so we constantly had to be aware of what he might be overhearing. All this was after the three months of torture that we had already endured, stretching our nerves and threatening our sanity when we didn't know if Julie was dead or alive.

We had been through so many emotions, sometimes even questioning our own judgement and wondering if perhaps we had got her wrong and Julie had just gone to London as the police believed. When I thought

like that I used to feel angry towards her for leaving
Kevin and expecting Charlie and me to just look after
him for her. But I still would have given anything for
that to be true, would have faced up to all the trouble
we would have been in for wasting police time, just to
have her safely back home again. Now that I knew for
sure she was dead I felt guilty for every moment I had
ever thought such things about her. How could I ever
have believed for a second that she would have left
Kevin?

Our doctor said that we really should tell Kevin the
truth about what had happened, but Andrew was
adamant that he didn't want to. Men always seem to
want to avoid talking about emotional things and in
hindsight it was a mistake, but at the time we just went
along with what Andrew wanted. He was Kevin's dad,
after all, so it was his decision. We concocted a story
between us that Julie had slipped in the bath because
there was no bathmat, hit her head and died. When we
told him she had gone to heaven he seemed to accept it,
and didn't ask anything about what had happened during the three months that she was missing. Time doesn't
mean much to small children; he had probably already
forgotten those months. Because he was only three, he
didn't question any of it.

On clear nights he would say, 'Come and look for me
mam,' and we would stand together by the window of

his bedroom, looking up at the sky, searching for the brightest star.

Now that I knew she was dead I wanted, more than anything else, to know who had killed my daughter and left my grandson without a mother to kiss him good-night and tuck him in. I wanted justice to be done.

Chapter Nine

Introducing Billy Dunlop

On 14 February 1990, less than two weeks after I found her body, the police arrested and charged a man called Billy Dunlop for our Julie's murder. When I heard his name, to start with I had trouble remembering exactly who he was, but then I realized he was a man I had met at Julie's house in the past. Julie knew a few of the lads that Andrew used to play football with. They all had nicknames they called one another and I didn't always know which one was which, or bother to find out. They were just there and I would chat to whoever I came across.

When I thought about it more deeply I could picture a couple of times he'd been in our Julie's house with other lads when we visited, but I couldn't say I knew anything about him. That situation would soon be remedied dramatically as the police, and everyone else we met who knew anything about him, filled us in with more stories about his past. The tales we were told painted an ugly picture of a side of local life I had previously known nothing about. I certainly hadn't realized that Andrew and Julie had been mixing with these sorts of men.

I could recall having a conversation with Billy Dunlop once about the Chinese restaurant in Billingham where I used to work on the cash desk. I remember a stocky man with dark hair and a moustache, who I later realized was Billy, sitting in Julie's kitchen and telling me he'd been there to the restaurant to eat. We chatted about it for a bit, but that was the only memory I had of ever talking to him at any length.

Even on that occasion he hadn't made a big impression, striking me as being quietly spoken and not at all aggressive or violent. In fact he didn't make much impact on me at all. It seemed that I had talked to the devil himself without even realizing what I was doing. Later I found out that he'd been brought up in the house next to the one I'd lived in all through my childhood. It's shocking how everyone ends up being connected to everyone else in a town like Billingham if you delve deep enough. It is also shocking how evil can so easily reside at the heart of a seemingly normal life. None of us ever knows what dark thoughts lurk in the hearts of our neighbours or the passers-by we see in the street, or what black deeds lie in their pasts.

Billy's best friend was a young man called Mark Ward. Mark was the boy who lived next door to 27 Grange Avenue with Kath, his mum, who was the woman I'd run to for help on finding the body. Mark was also the one who had received the call from the police about the anonymous tip-off. As I learned more and more of these facts, I struggled to piece them together in my head in order to try to make some sense of what might have happened that night, but none of it seemed to form a complete picture. There were too many missing pieces of the jigsaw for it to make any sense, too many pieces of misinformation.

Billy, I was told, had been living with his girlfriend Jayne, but they'd had a row a few months before and so at the time Julie was killed he'd been lodging with a mate of his called Don, at Don's house in the next road to Grange Avenue. Billy and Jayne had since made up and he had moved back in with her during the three months that Julie was presumed missing.

The day that Julie first disappeared, when I went next door the second time to ask Kath if she had seen or heard anything, Billy was actually sitting in the kitchen with Mark. Once again I didn't really take him in, being too distracted and worried, but when I thought about it later an image of him came back to me. That struck me as strange. If he was the murderer, why was he sitting there, cool as a cucumber the next morning? I certainly

113

don't think he said anything while I was in there or gave any indication that he might know where Julie had gone. I don't think he showed much interest in what I was saying at all. I was later told that this type of behaviour was typical of a psychopath – they often return to the scene of their crime – but at the time I thought nothing of it. I didn't really pay him any attention.

His name had first come to the police's attention during the three months when they thought Julie had simply run off to London. Officers had been making door-to-door enquiries around the neighbourhood, during which they had interviewed Billy and Mark Ward and Don, the lad Billy was lodging with.

Gradually we learned more and more from the police of what had happened on the night of the murder. A bunch of these lads, including Billy, had been to a stag night at the local rugby club. Billy and half a dozen of his mates apparently had a reputation for starting trouble wherever they went and were known locally as 'the Crazy Gang', a title they were proud to live up to at every opportunity. The police knew all about them, as did anyone who frequented the same pubs and clubs and had witnessed their rowdy behaviour.

Billy himself was well known around the area for being a 'hard man' and a lot of people were frightened of him. He was known to have convictions for violent assaults going back to 1975, when he was just a young lad growing up. There were many stories circulating about things he had done and things he was capable of, but it was hard to know how many of them were true and how many were myths. It was said he was shockingly violent, particularly when he was drunk, which was often. If you went into any of the pubs in old Billingham and just mentioned his name people would readily tell stories about him. He was the leader of the pack and had been since he was a kid.

One story that was widely told concerned the time he was trying to escape from some institution he'd been sent to when he was about sixteen. The police went looking for him and let a dog off the leash to track him down. People said that when the dog found him Billy turned round and cut the animal's head off with a knife. The tale had been told so many times it was impossible to know if it was true or not but it added to the aura of violence and fear that surrounded Billy wherever he went.

Andrew had been to school with him and said that even back then all the other kids were frightened of his bullying ways. Whether all the stories about Billy Dunlop were accurate or not, everyone in the area wanted rid of him, to see him safely behind bars, but most were too intimidated to speak up and the police never seemed to be able pin anything on him and make it stick.

This group of men, 'the Crazy Gang', often hired strippers for their rugby club stag dos and sometimes,

I'm told, the girls were more like prostitutes than dancers, willing to perform sex acts with the men on stage and that sort of thing. During the course of the evening at the club, while Julie was still at work delivering pizzas for 'Mr Macaroni' and Charlie and I were at home with Kevin, the story goes that Billy, fuelled up on a cocktail of drink, had dropped his trousers and exposed himself while trying to get up onto the stage with the stripper. He was showing off to his friends, trying to engage in sex acts. Egged on by his cronies who were just as drunk as he was, he frightened the girl half to death.

Drunk and dangerously sexually aroused, he started to cause so much trouble that the club doormen intervened and threw him out into the street after he had been involved in a fight with another man at the club. On the way out he head-butted the door in his rage and cut his eyebrow badly. By the time he got outside, his face streaked with his own blood, he was lathered up into such a fury that he attacked the man again knocking him to the floor. Billy beat him to the ground, ferociously punching him unconscious until the doormen were able to drag him off.

Once he had calmed down enough to realize he was covered in blood himself, Billy got someone to give him a lift to the local hospital to have his eyebrow stitched. I guess the doctors in casualty departments are used to seeing the results of pub brawls staggering through their doors in the small hours and just get on with patching them up and sending them on their way to sleep it off. I doubt they bother to ask many questions.

At about one-thirty in the morning Billy lurched back out of the hospital onto the streets, his cut stitched up but his frustration at having his evening of drunken fun interrupted still fermenting inside his head.

When the police arrived on Don's doorstep during the missing person enquiry he told them that Dunlop, who was lodging with him at the time, had returned home from the hospital at two o'clock in the morning, which wouldn't have left him with much time to get up to any serious mischief regarding Julie. If Don was telling the truth then Billy must have walked straight back home from the hospital and gone to bed. The police asked Don how he knew the time so precisely and he said his video clock was lit up beside the bed and he looked at it when Billy woke him up by coming in. In response to further questioning, Don told them that he'd heard Billy going straight to bed once he got in. That had been a good enough alibi for the police to move on to the next house on their list.

Once I found Julie's body and it changed from being a missing person's enquiry to a murder enquiry, the police went over all the previous statements and returned to see Don again, to check what he had told

them. This time, realizing things were a lot more serious than he had first imagined, Don changed his story.
He might have been willing to lie for Billy when the
police were just looking for a woman who had probably
gone off to London on her own, but he wasn't willing to
get himself implicated in a murder investigation. If he
had been caught lying in order to cover up for a murderer he could have ended up going inside himself. Even
Billy couldn't intimidate him to that degree. He admitted that Dunlop hadn't returned to the house at two
o'clock, as he had claimed before and that he was in fact
unaware of what time Billy had arrived back at his
lodgings. That left Billy potentially with several hours
of the night unaccounted for between leaving the hospital and arriving home, easily enough time to kill Julie
and clean the house up after him. If they had had their
suspicions about Billy before, the police were now sure
they were on the trail of their prime suspect.

They took out search warrants for Don's house and,
under the floorboards in the kitchen area of the lodgings
where Billy had been staying, they found Julie's missing
house keys. They were instantly recognizable because
they were attached to a big brass Playboy key ring that
she had brought back from London when she visited her
friend Margaret the year before.

The police found some of Dunlop's fingerprints on
the distinctive Playboy key fob, but that wasn't the only

evidence they were able to put together. The night that Julie was murdered Billy had been wearing a Billing-ham Rugby Club shirt and fibres from a shirt of that type had been found on the blanket that her body was wrapped in. There was also semen on the blanket that DNA testing showed could be his, together with human hairs.

'We haven't just got 100 per cent evidence that he's the guilty one,' the police assured us, 'we feel we've got a 110 per cent strong prosecution case.'

It seemed that they had redeemed themselves a little by conducting a fast and thorough murder investigation and catching the culprit almost immediately they had a body. There was some comfort for us in knowing who it was that we could hold responsible for taking our Julie from us, and in knowing that he would almost certain-ly be paying a just price for his crime. It didn't alleviate any of the pain of losing her, but it helped in the struggle to hold on to our sanity. We were beginning to be able to get a faint picture of what might have happened in and around Grange Avenue during the last hours of Julie's life, although we still didn't know how she had died.

We would have felt a great deal better, of course, if Billy Dunlop had come clean and admitted everything, but when he was arrested he denied the allegation, say-ing he had no idea how the keys could have got under his floorboards. He suggested that maybe someone was trying to frame him, even going to the trouble of planting his fingerprints on the brass fob. But such a blatantly ridiculous claim didn't rock the confidence of the police. They were sure they had their man and that he would be convicted at trial. It didn't seem likely that any jury would believe that someone could actually 'put' someone else's fingerprints on anything. It sounded laughable, like some sort of far-fetched plot line from a movie. The police were obviously relieved to be able to regain some of their reputation and also to think they were going to be able to get a man as dangerous as Billy Dunlop off the streets for a significant time.

Our liaison officer, Mark Braithwaite, was keeping Charlie and me updated on relevant developments as they happened, probably because the police were desperate to ensure they didn't let us down again as they had at the beginning of the investigation. I was grateful for that, even though I didn't always want to know every gory detail, like the fact that Julie's femur had been sent to one laboratory for examination and analysis, while her gullet had gone to another. It is very difficult to cope with the idea of your own child becoming no more than a selection of body parts to go under the knives and microscopes of a bunch of scientists you are never going to meet. Even then it was still better than not knowing what was going on. We really couldn't have faulted the murder squad for the meticulously considerate way they treated us during that stage of the investigation.

My biggest fear at that time was that Julie might still have been alive when Dunlop pushed her under the bath, and that he had left her there to die. The thought of her regaining consciousness and finding herself imprisoned behind a bath panel in an empty house, struggling in vain to escape while knowing she was going to die, kept going round and round in my head. But eventually the police were able to tell me categorically that she had been dead before he put her into that position. It's strange the things you can find scraps of comfort in when everything is so bleak.

The pathologist's report made it clear that the length of time Julie's body had lain undiscovered had made his job harder. There would have been a lot more evidence to tell us how she had died if the police had found the body when they first went into the house to search.

'The autopsy findings in this case,' the pathologist wrote, 'have been to a large extent obscured by quite advanced post-mortem changes.'

He concluded his report by saying it was not possible to state exactly what the cause of death had been.

'There was certainly no evidence of any natural disease to cause or accelerate death,' he wrote, 'and the circumstances and the presence of a violent sexual injury indicate that death must have been from other than natural causes. There was no evidence of a violent beating up and there were no broken bones. Given the negative findings and the general nature of the case it is likely that death has been due to some form of asphyxia, say strangulation or suffocation, and of course the subtle signs of these would easily be obscured by putrefactive change.'

Earlier in the report he had written in detail about the damage that had been done to Julie's vagina by whoever her killer was. To read and hear such things about your own child is unbearably painful, but I found my need to know the truth about what had happened to my baby was stronger than the revulsion I felt as more and more gruesome details came to light. I could hardly bear to think about it, but I still wanted to know everything.

'There was present,' the pathologist wrote, 'about the body only a single unequivocal injury. This consisted of a huge vertically running laceration running the whole length of the vagina posteriorly and on the left. This tear entered the peritoneal cavity. It represents the result of some extreme form of violence, such as the violent insertion of a foreign body into the vagina resulting in gross distension of the organ and subsequent tearing. Insertion of a fist or foot is less likely. The lesion could not have been caused by normal sexual intercourse and must be taken to be the result of a deliberate act of violence, perhaps even violation or defilement. It is possible that the injury occurred in life. If so it would cause pain, shock and heavy bleeding. It is only just possible that death could ensue acutely. It is more likely that the injury occurred after death however as an act of mutilation.'

In layman's terms, he seemed to be saying that whatever was done to her vagina probably wouldn't have killed her. The police had no idea what the instrument used for this terrible act might have been, and they didn't really know for sure if he had done it to her when she was alive or dead, although it was more likely that it happened after her death. Any mother stopping for a moment to think how they would feel to read such things about their daughter will be able to imagine just how I felt at that moment, but I was not going to allow my own horror to defeat me. I could not allow myself to shrink back from the truth and hide my head in the sand. I had to be able to cope with the information if I was going to make sure that Julie received justice for what had happened to her.

Mark Braithwaite explained that now the pathologists had finished with Julie's various body parts they had all been sent to the coroner, who would hold an inquest and then release the body for the funeral. I expect he thought it would be a relief to us to think that we would be moving forward, but it actually worried me.

'Have you got all the test results back?' I asked.

'We're just waiting for two more to come through,' he admitted.

I didn't feel too happy about that. What if we had Julie's remains cremated and the police then discovered that something had gone wrong with one of the tests? It would be too late by that time to do anything about it. I was absolutely paranoid about allowing anything to go wrong in the process of getting a guilty verdict for Billy Dunlop. If he was the guilty man I didn't want him to escape justice on some technicality just because we had rushed things at this stage. Charlie and I made an appointment to go and see the coroner with Mark and we told them both about our reservations.

'But the pathologists have finished with the body,' Mark protested. I suppose he thought that we would want closure on the whole business as quickly as possible, like most bereaved families.

'Listen, you,' I said, as firmly as I could manage. 'Your lot have cocked enough up. She's been dead since November and it's now April. A couple more weeks is going to make no difference to us or to Julie. I would prefer to wait until all the test results are back.'

The coroner looked at me over his glasses for a moment, and then turned to Mark. 'Mrs Ming isn't very happy about me opening the inquest,' he said, 'and neither am I. We will wait until all the results are back.'

Mark opened his mouth to protest.

'Shut up,' I rebuked him. 'Don't you say anything else.'

Eventually all the tests came back and the inquest could safely be held. We went along to listen to what they had to say. Even though I knew it would be painful, I wanted to know exactly what was happening and what was being said. I felt as though Julie needed to have a representative everywhere that her death was being discussed, and I knew Charlie and I would have to be the ones to do that. Besides, I was still finding that the only way to cope with my raw grief was by channelling it into action, so if there was anything at all I could usefully do, then I would do it.

The pathologist stood up and talked about his findings. As his words flowed round me, describing the most intimate details of Julie's corpse, I started to feel bad and then I suddenly found myself back in that bathroom. I couldn't see anything except a massive bath and Julie underneath it. I tried to blink the pictures away but they just became more vivid, the putrid smells filling my nostrils, making me gag. Terrified at having to relive the whole thing yet again I stood up and ran out of the room, but there was nowhere I could run to that would actually allow me to escape. Wherever I went the thoughts and pictures went with me inside my head and I knew they always would. But I couldn't let them frighten me off, any more than I could let Billy Dunlop's reputation for violence intimidate me. Julie needed us to stay on his trail and that was what we were going to do, however much we might prefer to just hide away behind our own front door and let the authorities deal with everything on our behalf. He was behind bars and it was my mission to keep him there.

Chapter Ten

The Funeral

Once the tests were done and the results were in there was no need for the authorities to keep hold of Julie's poor battered body any longer. She could finally be allowed some peace and dignity and we would have to face up to saying goodbye to her once and for all. The funeral directors brought the coffin to a funeral parlour in Middlesborough and phoned us to say she had arrived safely. Charlie and I went over, ringing Gary and Angela to tell them to meet us there.

The funeral directors respectfully showed us into the room where they had laid the coffin. I found it hard to breathe as my grief hit me full strength at the sight of it. It was yet another confirmation that she was gone, that we would never be able to speak to her again, never be able to say goodbye properly or tell her how much we loved her. It was all too late. The lid of the coffin was closed and I laid our flowers gently on the top. It felt a bit as though we were reclaiming her for the family after all the months she had spent away, being manhandled by strangers.

'I hope you're all right now, Julie,' I whispered, wondering whether there was a chance she might be able to hear me somewhere. 'I hope it's OK where you are.'

When Angela and Gary arrived it felt for a few minutes as if we were complete again, the whole family together in the same room for the first time since Julie had disappeared. It was almost like it used to be when the kids were all small and we were still able to offer them some parental protection against the dangers of the outside world, although the worst danger they'd had to face back then was the traffic on the main road outside the house. None of us wanted the moment to end, because we knew that once it was over we would never be together like that again; there would always be a part of us missing. All I had ever wanted was to have my family around me.

Eventually I knew it had to end and I forced myself to walk outside on wobbly legs to see the woman running the funeral parlour, tearing myself away from the coffin, moving as if I was in a trance. Following my lead, Angela offered to give Gary a lift back home, leaving Charlie in the room on his own with Julie. Only later did he tell me that once we had all gone he moved the flowers to one side and stretched himself over the lid in order to be close to her one last time.

'I promise you, Julie,' he whispered through the thick wood, 'that before I die I'll make sure I get the bastard who killed you.'

The funeral was booked for 20 April at St Mary's Church in Acklam. I went to see Dr Geoghegan the day before, hoping he could help me find a way to get through the ordeal.

'Do you know that song?' I asked him.

'What song?'

'The one that says "Make the world go away".'

'Yes,' he said, 'I know it.'

'Please can you give me some tablets to make tomorrow go away?'

'I wish I could,' he said, and I knew he meant it.

We decided to hold the service back in Acklam, even though we didn't live there any more, because it was the town where Julie had been born and brought up. It was where she had been to school and church and joined the Brownies and the Guides. Most of her good friends had come from there and most of the memories that all of us had of her were from the years we had spent there as a family. I wanted her school friends to be able to attend the service because I knew it would have meant a lot to her to know they cared. It wasn't that long, after all, since they had all been schoolchildren together.

Charlie, Gary, Angela, Andrew and I were picked up in a big black funeral car. As we drove past the old house where we used to live we turned to look out the windows and I voiced the thought that was going through all our heads.

'I wish we'd never moved from there,' I sighed. 'Maybe if we hadn't, then she would still be alive.'

I immediately wished I hadn't said anything because it made Andrew feel awful, as if we blamed it all on her meeting and marrying him. We never held anything against him, but we couldn't help thinking that if we had never moved to Billingham none of it would have happened and we would all still be together.

I had asked the people at the church to play 'Ave Maria' constantly through their sound system while the church was filling up, because it was such a beautiful song and because Julie had loved it so much. Hearing it reminded me of her wedding, the day when she was at her most alive and beautiful, when the future had seemed so full of promise for her and Andrew.

The church was already packed with friends and family as Charlie and I and the rest of the family walked slowly down the road towards it, following the coffin. I could see photographers from the papers standing around the bushes on the way through the churchyard, discreetly taking pictures, trying their best not to intrude. I didn't mind; I was in a different world anyway. They were nothing to do with what was going on inside my head.

I looked up at the coffin resting on the men's shoulders in front of us and pictured Julie's little body lying inside. It suddenly seemed all wrong. It should have been me in that box, not our Julie. Parents are supposed to die before their children. I wanted everything to stop, to change, to not be the way it was because it was too painful to bear. I wasn't sure I could take another step because every step I took was carrying me closer to the moment when I would have to say goodbye to her for ever, maybe leaving her on her own for all eternity.

A powerful wave of emotion that my subconscious must have been keeping a tight rein on for weeks rose up inside me, rushing up through my chest and into my head, cutting out all the sounds around me and bringing tears to my eyes. I was panicking at the thought of losing my child and being helpless to do anything about it. It's hard for any mother to endure the feeling of not being able to help their children when they need help. I started to scream, unable to hold the grief in, unable to control myself and maintain my composure for a second longer.

'Nobody would listen,' I sobbed. 'I told them she hadn't gone to London but nobody would listen.'

Charlie put his arm round me but there was nothing he could say. He was struggling to hold himself together and didn't have any strength left to help me. Somehow I kept walking, just planting one foot in front of the other, wailing as I went and hanging on to Charlie and his niece for support. Gary and Angela were behind us, with their partners.

As we drew closer to the church and to the moment when I would have to walk down the aisle through the crowd inside, I couldn't bear to go on. I was terrified of being trapped inside the church with all those eyes on me as I battled to hold myself together. I didn't know if I was going to be able to bear the pain of standing so close to the coffin while they played music and sang and talked about Julie. All my strength was draining away. I could hear the beautiful sounds of 'Ave Maria' floating out of the building and I could see in my mind a picture of our Julie and Andrew swirling round the dance floor at their wedding, so innocent and young and happy, with their whole lives ahead of them. But in front of me were the men carrying the box that contained the reality of what had happened to their dreams.

As the church doors loomed up before us I knew that once we were through them there would be no going back; Julie would be finally dead and gone. Even though I had known she was dead in my heart since she went missing the previous November, I had been able to hold on to a tiny scrap of hope for the first three months. After I found her body I had been so distracted with the details of the murder investigation, talking about Julie every hour of every day, that my grief had been put on hold. It had almost been as if she was still among us because the subject of her death so preoccupied us all. But now I was actually going to have to say goodbye to her and accept that I would never be seeing her again in this life. All my hopes had gone.

'I don't want to go in,' I told Charlie and his niece, feeling like a small child being asked to dive into the depths of a cold swimming pool. 'I can't do it.'

His niece took a firm hold of my arms and looked into my eyes. 'You've got to go in,' she said firmly. 'You've got to.'

She almost had to push me physically through the door. One of my colleagues from work told me a long time later how they had all been sitting in church, with the music playing around them, many of them remembering the wedding, and all of a sudden they heard a terrible noise at the entrance.

'It sounded like a child crying,' she told me. 'For a moment I thought you had brought Kevin with you. Then we realized it wasn't him crying, it was you. There was like this deathly silence and there wasn't a dry eye in the whole church. It was electrifying. The next moment you were in the church amongst us.'

Standing in those pews, with Julie lying a few feet away, I just wanted to hold her in my arms and never let her go. I felt as though my heart had finally broken and I didn't know how I would ever be able to cope with the pain.

After the service we went to the crematorium where I'd asked them to play Harry Secombe's 'I'll walk with God' on a continuous loop. I was adamant that I didn't want any lulls in the music, no uncomfortable silences. I wanted his voice ringing out all the time as Julie's body made its final journey through the curtains and out of sight. If she had had her way in the planning of the day we would probably have been listening to Boy George's 'Karma Chameleon'. People do that sort of thing these days but not back then, when they expected to hear 'suitable' music at funerals.

Finally it was all over. Julie had gone and Harry Secombe continued to sing as we made our way back out into the fresh air. The coffin had vanished and Julie was no more; the last sad scraps of her defiled earthly body had been disposed of. All that remained of her now was in our memories.

We had booked the Bluebell Hotel for tea and everyone went back there once we'd finished at the crematorium. The room was packed with dozens of familiar faces from Julie's past and as I looked around all I could think was that the only person who was missing was Julie herself. The rest of the day passed by in a blur of tears as well-meaning people tried their best to find the right words to say to me. It was a hopeless task because there were no right words. There was nothing that could be said that would comfort me at that moment.

The newspapers printed their pictures the following day under headlines like 'Family Farewell to Tragic Julie', and all I could think of when I looked at them was, what in God's name did Charlie's hair look like? He still had the curly perm that Julie had given him, but over the previous few months it had turned nearly white with grief. The wind outside the church had lifted it almost vertical and he looked like Don King the boxing promoter in his heyday.

'If Julie's looking down on us now,' Angela said when I showed her the pictures, 'she'd be saying "What on earth's happened to our Dad's hair?"'

Charlie just gave a thin smile and said nothing. Whatever was happening on the top of his head was the least of his problems.

Now, finally, I could start the grieving process. We bought a bench in Julie's name for the garden of remembrance where her ashes were scattered, and set about the task of fulfilling Charlie's final promise to her to make sure we got the man who had taken her young life so brutally. We had no idea what we were about to get ourselves into.

Chapter Eleven

Learning to cope

I worked for a health authority so my bosses were very understanding about how hard I was going to find coping with the return to 'normal' life after everything we had been through, but they also understood that it might help me to get back into the routine of it as soon as I could, in order to have at least some structure in my life.

Two days after I found Julie's body, my nurse manager suggested that I should go to see a staff psychologist who had recently been taken on. At first I wasn't sure that I felt ready to bare my soul to a complete stranger, but she was very insistent that it would do me good to talk to a professional.

'I've booked you an appointment to see Martin Bamber,' she told me. 'If you don't turn up I'll be coming to get you myself.'

I didn't know if that was the route I wanted to follow, but I knew I was going to have to do something if I wasn't going to go completely insane. I was constantly suffering from the most vivid and realistic flashbacks, unable to get the smell of Julie's body out of my nostrils. I couldn't shut my eyes to sleep because I would immediately see her under the bath and I was in danger of collapsing from the mixture of stress and exhaustion if I kept on trying to cope with it all on my own.

I was shocked by how young Martin Bamber looked when I walked into his office for our first appointment. He seemed like an academic type with mousy hair and little round frameless glasses. I soon discovered he was still only in his twenties and I wasn't sure that I was going to be able to talk frankly to a man so much younger than myself, but I knew I had to try.

'I only know a bit about the case,' he told me as we settled down, 'because I've just moved to the area, so if you'd like to tell me what happened in your own words that would be very helpful.'

I didn't want to be rude since he'd been kind enough to give up his time for me, so I took a deep breath and started talking. Three hours later I was still there and still talking. He was the easiest person in the world to communicate with and I went on seeing him for three or four years after that. He was absolutely brilliant at helping me to analyse everything that was going on inside my head. Martin was able to explain so much to me about why I felt the way I did, why I acted the way I did and what I needed to do in order to find enough peace inside my head and my heart to be able to overcome the pain and carry on living as near to normal a life as possible.

The nights were always the worst times. Unable to sleep, with thoughts of what might have happened to Julie during her last hours swirling round and round in my head, I wouldn't be able to lie in bed for long. I often got up and start doing housework in the small hours of the morning to try to distract myself, even though there was seldom anything that needed to be done. I just had to keep my mind busy with trivia, so that it couldn't dwell on the many questions that still had no answers.

Although Julie had finally been laid to rest and we had said our last goodbyes, we still had Dunlop's trial to go through, so there was no chance of being able to forget what had happened for even a few minutes at a time.

Lack of sleep was making everything worse, stretching my nerves like brittle elastic, taking them dangerously close to breaking point. My behaviour was damaging my relationship with Charlie as well. He was dealing with his grief differently to me, blocking the memories, forcing them to the back of his mind. I couldn't understand how he was able to do that, any more than he could understand why I couldn't. It was then that Martin introduced me to the term 'psychic numb-ing', and explained that this was what was making me feel emotionally detached from other people. He told me that was why my relationship with Charlie was deterio-rating. I simply wasn't able to cope with it.

I wanted to be able to move on and recover for the sake of everyone else in the family as well as for myself, but I didn't seem able to do it. It was as though I was stuck in a time warp, where I wasn't being of any use to anyone, not even Julie. Neither Charlie nor I were left with the necessary spare emotional capacity to help one another.

'It's time you put it out of your mind,' Charlie would say to me every time I woke after a nightmare or flash-back.

'Do you think I want to keep seeing and smelling Julie?' I would shout back furiously, even though I knew none of it was his fault and that he was suffering just as much as I was, only in a different way.

My erratic behaviour was driving him mad and the strain between us was threatening to split us up, if only to give us each a little peace and space from one another. I've been told that as many as nine out of ten couples end up apart after losing a child to murder and I can quite believe it. Men and women handle their grief in such dif-ferent ways it's hard for them to stay together in such stressful circumstances and most don't have the strength to even try by that stage. If all your energy is going into holding on to your own sanity, it is hard to pay attention to repairing a damaged relationship.

Charlie never underestimated what I had been through. He always told me that if he had been the one to find Julie's body he was sure he would have dropped dead on the spot. 'I couldn't have lived to tell the tale,' he would say.

Over the years we've been to a lot of conferences about bereavement together, searching for any crumbs of comfort we can find and pleased to share our experiences with others if they can be of any help. It is always comforting to be with people who understand exactly how you feel and what you have endured. At one event there was a vicar and his wife, whose daughter had hung herself. The wife spoke about how she thought her husband was cold and believed he was not grieving for their daughter whereas she was having friends over, talking about it and crying openly. One day, she told us, she came home early from shopping and found her husband sitting in their daughter's bedroom with her ballet music blaring from the sound system. He was holding a picture of the girl and crying. That, she discovered, had been his weekly routine ever since their daughter had died. It was his way of coping with the grief, like an emergency valve regularly letting out the steam that was constantly building up inside him. I heard many stories after that of how men would cry in private, in the shower or sitting in their cars with the music on, and I have been moved to understand how deeply fathers love their children, even if they are often unable to show it in the same way as the women.

Gary and Angela both reacted more like Charlie than like me, neither of them wanting to talk about how they felt, keen to block the pain out as quickly as possible. I think maybe it brought them a bit closer to each other; perhaps they talked about things together that they didn't share with me in case they upset me more.

When I was about to sort through Julie's clothes one day, Angela stopped me, whipping them all away.

'You don't need to have bags of old clothes to remember Julie,' she said firmly. 'You're just getting morbid.' And she was right but I wouldn't have been able to throw them away myself.

However quiet they were on the outside, I knew Angela and Gary were both hurting inside. Gary did tell me that he blamed himself because he hadn't gone round to her house that night. If he'd been there, it wouldn't have happened. I think he struggled with his guilt about that for a while – but we all had something we regretted not doing. If only I had talked her into coming back to stay at my place that night, it wouldn't have happened either. We each dealt with our feelings separately, in different ways.

One unexpected beneficial side effect to come from the adrenaline surge that the shock caused in me was that it seemed to cure the asthma attacks I used to get as a young woman. I had always had to carry around an inhaler but I never needed it again after the day I found Julie's body. The day after the discovery the chest specialist at the hospital very kindly rang me to offer his condolences and to say that if I had any problems to come straight to his clinic and not worry about making an appointment. Apparently, he told me, the effect could have gone the other way and the shock could have made the asthma worse. I suppose if I'd started having panic attacks that could have brought on asthma attacks as well.

Eventually the stresses of living together with our grief became too much for Charlie and me. We both needed to be on our own for at least a few hours each day, so he stayed in the house and I rented another place while we both tried to sort out our feelings and find a way of coping.

By then Martin had explained to me that I was suffering from post-traumatic stress disorder while Charlie was suffering from severe depression, and it was just too much for us to be together under the same roof. I was back at work in the hospital by then. I would come in from a hard day and Charlie would be going on and on about Dunlop until I thought my head was going to

143

explode. Meanwhile I would want to talk about Julie and about how I felt but he was unable to listen to me. It was all part of the way he was handling losing Julie but I wasn't in a fit state to be able to cope with it. In 1991, while Billy was on trial, Charlie's depression got so bad that he was admitted to a psychiatric ward for a couple of months, where they helped him to deal with his stress. No one who hasn't experienced it can imagine how much damage bereavement like ours does to a family.

Underneath it all our marriage must have been very strong, because even though we didn't live together for a year, we would still see each other every day. At least it meant that we didn't have to worry about disturbing and distressing one another at night. We had been together for so long it was hard to be apart, almost like losing another part of ourselves. I felt as though I couldn't live with Charlie, but at the same time I couldn't live without him. I felt furious that Dunlop had been able to do so much harm to my family beyond the obvious damage he did to Julie herself. It was as though there was no answer to any of our problems, no solution that would ever make things right again, nothing that could bring things back to how they were when we were all together as a family.

I was still filled with so much anger towards the police for the way in which they had messed up the whole investigation that sometimes it was hard to contain it, and the flashbacks would never leave me alone.

'I want you to physically go back to that bathroom in Grange Avenue,' Martin told me a few months after I started seeing him. 'I think confronting your fears will really help you to move on.'

Go back? But in my head I was going back there all the time; that was exactly the problem I was trying to cure. I knew he had been right about other things before and he deserved my trust, so I agreed to do as he asked.

'All right,' I said. 'I'll do it.'

Mark Braithwaite, the police liaison officer, realized how frightened I was at the thought of revisiting the scene of all my worst nightmares and agreed to come with me. The council hadn't allocated the house to anyone else yet and we still had the keys. I was quite calm as we drove into Grange Avenue and pulled up outside, but when we walked through the door and I saw the stairs stretching up in front of me I felt a terrible shudder of fear pass through me. Was this really going to help? Or was it just going to prove to be the last straw, tipping me over the edge into insanity once and for all?

'Can I hold your hand?' I asked Mark.

'Of course,' he replied, kindly.

Holding on tightly like a little girl on her way to the dentist or on her first day at school, I climbed the stairs with him, then paused outside the bathroom door so that I could gather my strength for the final steps.

'Do you want me to come in with you?' he asked.

'No,' I said, 'just leave me. You go down. I'll be all right.'

I waited till he had disappeared from sight before taking a deep breath and stepping through the door into the empty room. The police had stripped the bath and the panel out and sent them off to Birmingham for some sort of laser tests, so it looked more like a building site than Julie's home. My knees wobbled and refused to support me. I sank down onto the floor, leaned back against the wall, and felt as though my heart was breaking. I waited for my breathing to steady itself and then looked around, taking in every detail, trying to force out the old pictures and replace them with new ones from the scene in front of me, pictures of an empty, harmless room.

In the corner of the floor was a stain where Julie's body fluids had seeped into the floorboards over the three months and the only thing I could think about was all the long days and nights she had lain there without us knowing anything about it, murdered and abandoned and alone. I pictured all the policemen coming and going on the other side of that flimsy panel while she lay there, twisted and still, the last of her life's juices ebbing out of her. I remembered standing there with Angela, talking to the police about her, looking through her makeup bag, when all the time she was lying just inches away.

Mark waited patiently for me downstairs until I felt calm enough to pull myself back onto my feet and leave the room forever.

Martin had been right because although it was a painful experience to go through, the next time I had a nightmare I saw Julie actually walking away with a bath panel under her arm.

'You've moved on in leaps and bounds,' he said when I told him, 'because you're not stuck under the bath any more.'

While Dunlop was in Durham Prison on remand Gary found out that another lad he knew was in there too and arranged to go and visit him. He and Charlie cooked the whole thing up between them, and went into the prison together. Charlie says he wanted Dunlop to see him, wanted him to know that we were not going to just go away and leave it all up to the police, that we were after him and that we wouldn't rest until he was behind bars for what he had done to our child. It was part of the promise Charlie had made to our Julie when she was lying in her coffin.

When they got back home from the visit they told me they'd seen Dunlop across the visiting room and they knew he had seen them too, but they hadn't spoken to him. I don't think I would have been able to do that at that stage. I think I would have lost my self-control and gone flying across the room at him. The wardens would have been struggling to pull my fingers off his throat. We later heard that the sight of Charlie sitting there, staring at him, had rattled Dunlop badly. I dare say it reminded him of stories he would have heard as a boy about the powers of the inscrutable Chinamen with their knives and their opium and their 'slow boats to China'.

There was always a lot of local media interest in the story of Julie's death and at one stage Billy Dunlop's dad agreed to come forward and talk about his son for a television documentary. He maintained that he didn't believe Billy had killed our Julie because, as he told the cameras, strangling 'wasn't Billy's style'. His dad said that if Billy ever killed someone he would do it by 'battering them' to death. I found it hard to understand why any father would want to appear on television and say something like that, as if somehow that made his son out to be a better person than everyone was saying.

He openly admitted that he had always brought up his children to stand up for themselves in fights. He claimed that he had taught them to box and to obey the rules, but that even as a boy Billy had never known where to draw the line when it came to fighting back. Most people, he suggested, would just knock their opponent down and consider they'd won the fight, but once his opponents were on the floor Billy would keep on kicking and beating them until his temper was spent. That certainly bore out eyewitness reports of what had happened to the man who Billy had attacked outside the rugby club. Maybe something similar had happened to Julie, even if there hadn't been any evidence of a beating.

The more we learned about Billy Dunlop the more we believed he was a danger to society and the more determined we became to have him convicted and imprisoned. His killing of Julie had obviously not been one isolated act of madness, but an inevitable consequence of all the patterns of behaviour that he seemed to consider normal.

Winning justice for Julie had become the main focus of our lives, giving us a reason to keep going. We planned to follow Billy Dunlop's case every inch of the way until he was convicted. We wanted to do everything we could to ensure that he was given a sentence that fairly befitted his crime. At least now we had a focus for our lives, something proactive we could do for our child.

Chapter Twelve

The Police
complaints Authority

We launched an official complaint against the police force while the internal investigation into the Cleveland police force was still under way. It was based on the list of grievances I wrote out the night after I found Julie, when I was still in the initial stages of shock and anger and included everything from the moment we first went to the police to report Julie missing and the night that Charlie and Gary were arrested for making a scene at the pizza shop.

The investigation took a few months and then the Deputy Chief Constable Jack Ord had to write a report to the Police Complaints Authority in London on the findings, giving the reasons why they had failed to find Julie. As soon as they published it we were sent a copy and when I read it I couldn't believe my eyes. It seemed to me to be an absolute whitewash. The following is the

letter that we were sent by the Police Complaints
Authority on 17 September 1990:

Dear Mr and Mrs Ming,
I am writing on behalf of the Police Complaints Authority
about the complaints you made on 6 February 1990.
Before discussing those complaints, however, I want
you to know how sorry we are about the tragic death of
your daughter and the way in which subsequent
circumstances added to your grief.

You will recall that Captain Taylor wrote to you on
14 June 1990, after receiving the report of the
investigation into your complaints about the conduct of
officers of Cleveland Constabulary to say that the
Authority were satisfied that the investigation had been
carried out properly. I believe that he has also explained
to you that the Authority's other task is to consider the
disciplinary aspects of the case. I enclose a note which
explains our independent role in the complaints
procedure and some of the factors which we have to
take into account before reaching a decision.

Clearly, your greatest concern is that the police
failed to find Julie's body. The investigation into your
complaints has found that her disappearance was in
fact taken extremely seriously from the outset and a
large number of officers were involved at one time or
another. You have complained about the attitude of

some of them. For instance, you believed that the
woman constable, to whom you first reported that Julie
could not be found, showed little interest – an attitude
underlined by the fact that she continued to chew gum.
She admits that she chews dental gum occasionally but
the records show that she dealt with the matter
meticulously and diligently. Accordingly, the complaint
about her cannot be substantiated. As to the officer
who you alleged made a distasteful remark, he insists
that he did not intend to offend and he thinks it possible
that you took his comment out of context. We note that
he apologized to you later for inadvertently causing you
distress and we believe the matter should rest there.
We take the same view about your complaint about the
officer from the Community Relations Department. He
has been interviewed and regrets that his attempts to
reassure you were construed as implying that he did not
recognize and believe your concern. He says that in
fact he was disturbed by Julie's disappearance but
despite his own reservations, tried to give you some
hope that the matter would be happily resolved.

Your complaint that information was improperly
disclosed to Mark Ward could not be investigated fully,
owing to the reluctance of the witness to assist.
However, the limited investigation which was carried
out revealed no evidence to substantiate this
allegation.

Your arrest, Mr Ming, and that of your son were justified on the evidence available at the time but the investigation has shown that the period you both spent in custody was excessive. Your complaint in this respect is substantiated as is your complaint that the enquiries into the alleged assault were not satisfactorily concluded and communicated. However, the investigation of your complaint that you were left in a cold cell with no blanket has found no evidence that the heating system was malfunctioning during the time of your detention and your custody log indicates that in fact you slept well.

As to your complaint, Mr Ming, about Detective Sergeant Kramer, he says that he passed on the information you gave and tried to reassure you, despite your criticism of his colleagues, that the case was being handled properly. We note that you subsequently apologized to him for being 'hot headed' and that he, in turn, apologized for his remark.

But to return to the Police's failure to find your daughter's body, the investigation into your complaint found that the endeavours of many officers to find her came to naught because of a basic failure of communication between those concerned. They, and the Force in general, are well aware that the result both showed the Force in a poor light and added considerably to your distress. The Deputy Chief

Constable has told the Authority that valuable lessons have been learned and that, while he does not consider that the officers concerned were guilty of neglect, he is disappointed with their performance. He does not think that formal disciplinary charges should be brought but he has made the following discipline-related proposals:

- That two detective inspectors, who between them must take full responsibility for the failure to discover Julie's body, should be seen by their respective Divisional Commanders and be given strong advice;
- That two inspectors should be seen by their Divisional Commander and strongly advised as to their responsibility when reviewing prisoners' detention;
- That two custody sergeants should be seen by their Divisional Commander and reminded in strong terms of their role and responsibilities within the Custody Office;
- That a detective constable should be advised by his Divisional Commander with regard to his failure to resolve earlier his investigation of the allegation against Mr Ming and his son of assault and damage, and to notify them of the outcome. This matter will also be brought to the notice of Divisional Commanders.

I should explain that 'advice' is a disciplinary term used by the police and is neither given nor received lightly.

The Deputy Chief Constable has also asked the Authority to convey to you his sincere condolences in your time of grief together with his deep regret at Julie's death and the failure to discover her body.

The Authority have carefully considered all the papers contained in the report of the investigation and have concluded that the evidence is not sufficient to justify formal disciplinary charges against any officer.

However, we have decided that the Deputy Chief Constable's proposals are the most appropriate way of responding to your complaints.

Yours sincerely,
G. V. Marsh
Member of the Authority

The official line, therefore, was that the reason why they had failed to find Julie's body was 'lack of communication' between the forensic officers inside the house. Hard as it was to understand how five grown men could fail to communicate effectively in such a small space, it seemed to us he was saying that each of the officers in the team thought someone else had searched the bathroom and the loft properly, so didn't bother to do it themselves. Having worked out that in their opinion that was all that had gone wrong, it was then decided that no one was going to be sacked. All that was going to happen was the officers concerned would be given 'strong advice' – whatever that meant. Detective Inspector Lee, who had been in charge of the investigation, actually went on to be promoted, eventually becoming the Commander of Stockton police force.

If I had been angry with them before reading the report, I was even more furious afterwards. In fact I was so angry I wasn't willing to just let it go. I asked our solicitor to write to the Deputy Chief Constable and request a meeting. I wanted to be able to sit round a table with all the forensic officers and have them explain to me personally what the hell they had been doing in that house for five days, apart from 'not communicating'. Had they just been humouring me all that time? Were they so certain that Julie had disappeared off down to London, leaving her child behind, that they all sat round the kitchen table playing cards for five days? (Apart from one man sticking his head through the loft hatch, of course.) I wanted to hear some straight, honest answers, not read some official report designed to cover everyone's backs.

Our solicitor received a formal reply from the Deputy Chief Constable saying that he could not agree to meet with us. As the matter was dealt with by the Police Complaints Authority, it would not be appropriate for him to discuss these issues. This seemed like yet another slap in the face, suggesting that they thought I was little more than a mad, bitter, paranoid woman, hell bent on wasting as much police time as possible just to satisfy my own lust for revenge.

Incensed, I told a local journalist who had been very helpful and had kept in regular touch from the beginning, that we were thinking of suing Cleveland Police. He must have passed that comment on – maybe he asked the police for their reaction – because the same day the police commander rang and asked to come and see us. It seemed that journalists could get action from public officials that the rest of us could only dream of, even if you were the victim's mother.

'I'd rather have talked to the organ grinder,' I replied grumpily to the commander, 'but since they're only sending the monkey, you'd better come.'

Despite this put-down, the poor chap still turned up and he must have been expecting the worst. No one in that police force could have been in any doubt about how angry I was by then. I'm sure they were all swapping horror stories about me and the way I refused to give up and disappear quietly. Looking back, I feel sorry for that commander but at the time I was so stressed out and medicated I wasn't in a mood to show any of them any mercy. He had walked straight into the lions' den.

'Nobody would ever say you weren't entitled to compensation for what you have suffered,' he assured us.

'But compensation isn't going to bring our daughter back,' I reminded him, 'is it?'

'We've been made to look very foolish in this case,' he admitted.

'You've been made to look complete idiots,' I agreed. 'I didn't even speak to the press initially; it was you who made the big headlines about how you were sending out divers to the pond and dogs onto the surrounding wastelands around Billingham. I've always believed in the afterlife, and so did our Julie. If she's watching us from up there she'll be saying that if you spent less money on the police benevolent fund and just supplied your forensic officers with National Health glasses you might have done better.'

I could see how uncomfortable I was making him feel and I did start to feel sorry for him because it wasn't as if he had been one of the officers on the case and at least he'd had the guts to come and talk to us. Charlie was giving me a look that suggested I should shut up now but I was on a roll, really wanting to get to the Deputy Chief Constable so I could tell him personally what I felt about his report.

After this meeting, once they realized I wasn't going to go away, Cleveland police offered us £5,000 compensation, which sounded to me like a bit of an insult. Our solicitor was keen for us to take it, saying that it was very rare for the police to even admit they were in the wrong, let alone offer compensation, but I still refused. After all, they could hardly deny they had been in the wrong, considering the evidence – we actually had a dead body to prove just how wrong they had been. The next offer was £10,000 and although it still didn't seem like the right sort of amount to compensate us for everything they had put us through I was too stressed to carry on with the fight. I wanted it all to end, so I gave in to our solicitor and accepted. I told myself that at least they had admitted publicly that they had done wrong and that they had a case to answer to. Looking back now I think I should have held out a bit longer, but even I had to take advice from professionals occasionally.

We also got some money from the Criminal Injuries Compensation Authority – £15,000, which was supposed to compensate me for having post-traumatic stress disorder and Charlie for having severe depression. There was no satisfaction in any of this, though. What we really wanted was to watch Billy Dunlop being found guilty of Julie's murder and sentenced to life. Only then would it feel as though we could start to move on and rebuild our lives.

Chapter Thirteen

The Trial

The trial of Billy Dunlop started in May 1991, eighteen months after Julie was killed. It felt as though we had been waiting for that day to come forever. As we walked up the steps to the court we came face to face with Derrick Dobson, the senior investigating officer in the case, for the first time. He came over and introduced himself to us.

'At last,' I said, 'we get to meet the "hunter".' I couldn't resist reminding him of the way in which he had styled himself on the television. Since he had managed to find and charge Billy within two weeks of knowing that Julie had been murdered, I couldn't claim that he hadn't done his job properly.

By the time we actually walked into the courtroom I could barely remember what our lives had been like before it all started. What did I used to think about all

161

day before my mind was filled with flashbacks and police enquiries and so much anger and sadness? It was as if we were all different people, our lives changed forever by someone else's few moments of insanity.

Although I was nervous about standing up in front of a packed courtroom as a witness, and terrified about having to listen to every detail of what had happened to Julie that night, I was also relieved to think that we might finally be approaching some sort of closure. Once it was over and Billy had been convicted, I thought, I would feel that we had succeeded in getting some justice for Julie and we could all concentrate on trying to get on with repairing our own lives. I knew I would never forget her, or the way in which she had died, but I was very conscious that I had two other children and it wasn't fair that their lives should be blighted forever by what had happened to Julie. We had to be able to put her death behind us and turn our thoughts to the living, and this trial would be the way to do that.

The trial was being held in front of a judge called Swinton Thomas, at Moot Hall in Newcastle, a famous old courthouse down by the river. The case went on for three weeks and was the most gruelling experience imaginable. When Dunlop was brought into the courtroom on the first day, I felt physically sick. I stared hard at him, trying to see inside his mind. I was thinking about the fact that he's the only person who knows exactly how Julie died, what she said in her last moments, and how quickly it was all over. Did he have any idea of the trauma he had put my whole family through? Did he ever think about that? There was no sign of it. He sat in the dock with a fixed expression that never changed throughout the trial, not an ounce of emotion visible.

Giving evidence and having to relive those early terrible months was like a waking nightmare. The defence barrister kept asking me for more and more detail, making me search further and further into my memory, digging up facts I had chosen to bury deep, bringing the scene more and more alive inside my head.

'When you went into the bathroom, Mrs Ming,' he would ask, 'and you put your hand behind the bath panel, was it your left hand or your right hand?'

As I struggled to remember and answer correctly I was transported back in flashbacks so lifelike that the smell of Julie's body filled my nostrils all over again. It was as if I was actually standing in the bathroom that I had hoped I had put behind me forever, the room that still had the bath and the body in it. The pictures were so vivid I couldn't see the courtroom at all; all reality had disappeared from in front of my eyes, leaving me in some dreadful, dark, haunted corner of my own memory. I forced myself to remain there, listening to the questions, trying to answer them without crying or fainting.

When I was back sitting in the gallery again, listening to other people talking about Julie, it was just as painful. It's hard to hear someone you love being discussed in a courtroom. She was our baby, our Julie, so how come these people knew things about her that we didn't? The facts sounded so cold, the descriptions so matter of fact. I remembered Julie as the mop-haired little angel I had given birth to and the pretty little girl who liked to dance and do gymnastics and dress up in strange clothes. But these men were discussing the sexual habits and morals of a grown woman, making assumptions about her, judging her, making it sound as if she was the criminal on trial, rather than the innocent victim.

I didn't recognize the woman the lawyers and witnesses were describing as the same person as the Julie in my memory and in my heart. Once children become sexually active they seldom share the details with their mothers. Even though I used to see Julie every day and we talked about everything under the sun, I hadn't realized that she had started seeing other boys since her relationship with Andrew had begun to fail. But now I was being forced to sit there and listen to every liaison in clinical detail, as if they were crimes she had committed, proof that she deserved to be killed, as if it was her fault in some way that Dunlop had lost control that night.

It wasn't just that I didn't like to have to listen to details about Julie's life, which I believed were her own private business; I also hated the thought that other people were hearing them and would be making judgements about her, people who had never met her while she was alive, who knew nothing about her beyond what they had heard in court. They didn't know anything about what sort of child she was, what sort of granddaughter, daughter and mother; they only knew about her as the victim of a violent and sadistic murderer.

I had to admit it sounded as though she had been careless and foolish with her affections, but having it spelled out to me was yet another shock to my already battered system. Listening to everyone talking about her, I suddenly realized why the Iranians at 'Mr Macaroni' had been so evasive when Charlie and I turned up and started asking questions; they must have known something about her private life and thought we had come that day as irate parents trying to find out who had been messing around with their daughter.

The biggest shock was to find that Julie had actually slept with Dunlop once, some time before. The court was told that Dunlop had gone back to see her on a later occasion, about ten days before she died. After that meeting a friend claimed that it was almost as if Julie had changed personality overnight, as if she was absolutely terrified of something. What could he have said to her or done to her on that visit to make her so frightened? Why hadn't she come to Charlie and me for help? Why hadn't she confided in me? It was as if they were describing the life of someone I didn't know at all.

I was so exhausted from the stress of everything we had been through, and so heavily medicated, that the following three weeks in the courtroom passed almost as though they were happening to someone else. I watched most of the proceedings from the public gallery through a fog of shock, noticing strange little details like the three jurors who appeared to sleep through virtually the whole trial. It was worrying me that they didn't seem to be paying attention but, I told myself, the case was so cut and dried maybe they had all made up their minds that he was guilty already and didn't feel they needed to hear any more. They were just going through the motions and all we had to do was endure it and then he would be sentenced. It still seemed disrespectful to Julie that they couldn't even be bothered to stay awake.

Jayne, the girlfriend who Billy had moved back in with after Julie's death, arrived in court looking threatening and tough, as if she had deliberately got herself up to look like a hard man's moll. Her hair was all spiked up aggressively and her ears were full of piercings. I'd heard about her from other people who'd been at school in her year and they all said she hadn't been like that till she met Dunlop, that she had been really nice and then she had changed, as if to please him.

After all the details of the medical evidence had been heard I felt sick and had to go outside for some air, leaving Charlie to follow what was happening for both of us for a while. We had a volunteer victim support officer who sat with us in court and she came out at the same time as me to go to the toilet. I was sitting alone in the corridor, trying to gather my composure, when I heard the door to the court-room open and saw that Jayne had followed me out. I averted my eyes, not wanting to provoke a confrontation.

'You must hate me,' she said and I knew she was talking to me.

'Why would I hate you?' I asked, too weary to fight with anyone else. 'I don't even know you. But I hate the man you live with.'

She sat down next to me uninvited.

'I've got two children to him,' she said, 'and they keep asking me when their daddy's coming home.'

'At least he's going to be coming home one day,' I reminded her. 'My daughter is never coming home.'

'I didn't want to believe he'd done this,' she went on as if she hadn't heard me. 'But it sounds from all the evidence like he did.'

'He's an absolute psychopath,' I said. 'What's he gained by doing this?'

She shrugged, obviously having no more understanding of what had happened than I did. I began to realize she was as much his victim as the rest of us.

167

'Didn't you notice anything different in his behaviour during the three months before I found Julie's body?' I asked.

'I've tried to think about that time,' she said. 'The only thing I remember is that because I knew Julie I was scanning the local paper every night for news about her. If there was anything there I would read it out to him, but he never once made any comment or read anything about her for himself. I thought nothing of it at the time, but when he was charged I started thinking about it.'

At that moment the victim support woman came back from the bathroom and Jayne didn't say any more. For the first time I wondered what sort of life she must have been being forced to live with such a frightening, violent man.

It was only once the case came to court that we found out more about what had happened in the five days that the police were inside the house in Grange Avenue. When the officer who said he had checked the loft was called to the witness stand he admitted all he had actually done was stand on the banister, push his head through the hatch, strike a match and look around. Satisfied there was no body up there he closed the hatch, jumped down off the banister and left it at that.

'Are you still employed by the Cleveland Constabulary?' the examining lawyer enquired, obviously having trouble believing what he was hearing.

'Oh, yes,' the policeman replied innocently, as if such gross negligence was just another normal occurrence in his working day.

We also discovered that the alarm the police had installed when they left the house hadn't malfunctioned at all. It had actually rung in the police station when the intruder got in the day after the police had gone. Two officers had reached the house within four minutes of the alarm going off. When they got there they could see no sign of forced entry but the back window was standing wide open. The television was on the draining board in the kitchen and the video had been stolen.

They'd radioed for a police dog handler to come to the house. The dog went all round the downstairs and came up with nothing. As the handler started to go up the stairs the dog had become highly agitated, although it didn't bark. It dragged its handler into the bathroom and became even more excited but because it still didn't bark he decided to pull it out of the bathroom and take it into the garden to search for intruders there. The dog was trained to bark when it smelled a live person, not a dead body.

I couldn't believe what I was hearing as the dog handler described the scene. It was all I could do to stop myself shouting down at him: 'You bloody idiot!' If his dog was agitated in the bathroom, why didn't he try to find out what had caused it?

One of Billy's claims was that he had got so drunk at the rugby club he hadn't any idea what he was doing after that, which I suppose he hoped would excuse any discrepancies in his story. Wandering around the town drunk gave him a sort of alibi for the lost six hours, or at least a possible explanation. The police, however, had found the doctor in the accident and emergency department at the hospital who had stitched the cut in his eyebrow that night, before Billy went round to Julie's street. When they called the doctor to the witness stand he said that although Billy had obviously had a few drinks by the time he got to casualty, he wasn't out of control in any way and would have been perfectly capable of remembering what he was doing after leaving the hospital. He said he could be sure of that because he had given Billy some anaesthetic for the stitches and he would have judged how much to give him by how much alcohol Billy had in his blood at the time.

'If he had been blind drunk,' he explained, 'I wouldn't have administered any anaesthetic.'

As I listened to the evidence more pieces of the story fell into place for me, gradually bringing a picture of what had happened into focus. I realized that Billy had been sitting on the other side of the wall in the house

170

next door with his friend Mark for much of the time that the forensic team were supposedly pulling Julie's home to pieces in their search for clues. I could only imagine what must have been going on in his head through those five days. He must have been mystified as to why they hadn't found the body, because he knew he'd left it behind the bath. He must have been expecting any minute to hear shouting and sirens and see a flurry of activity in the street outside as the police realized they were dealing with a murder case. As every day passed without incident he was probably beginning to distrust his own memory, wondering if he had dreamed the whole thing, wondering if he was going mad.

The police believe it likely that once Dunlop knew the forensic team had left the house he went back in during the night, using Julie's keys, to see if her body was still where he'd put it. That could explain the mysterious burglary, when the video disappeared and the television was found in the kitchen by the open window. By doing that he made it look as though it was a simple break-in and attempted burglary, in case anyone saw him coming or going. His visit must have been very fast if the police got there as quickly as they said they did. He certainly wouldn't have had time to move the body somewhere safer, even if he had wanted to.

Every hour of the day and night my brain was churning over all the new facts and theories that were being produced in the courtroom, trying to make sense of them, trying to understand what had happened and why, trying to work out what effect each revelation might have on the eventual sentence that Dunlop received.

It seemed that the night that he killed Julie he must have stayed around afterwards to tidy the house and cover his tracks, leaving it in the pristine state Gary and I found it in the next day. It's possible that he might even have still been inside the house the next morning when I first came round to wake Julie up at seven-thirty, since he didn't get back to his lodgings with Don till after that time (according to the evidence presented in court). It was unlikely he would have been wandering the streets unnoticed, or would have gone anywhere else between leaving Julie's and getting back home.

'It's lucky you didn't have a key to let yourself in,' one policeman told me, 'because if he was still there he would probably have killed you and Kevin as well. He would have needed to eliminate you as potential witnesses.'

It was terrifying to think how close I could have been to catching Billy red-handed that morning. Was he really still cowering behind closed curtains as I banged on the doors and shouted through the letterbox? Was he sitting in there as impassively as he was now sitting in the dock, staring straight ahead, just waiting for me to give

172

up and go away? Did he know that I didn't have a key or was he standing behind the door, waiting to pounce the moment I came in? Would he have strangled us too, or stabbed us, or beaten us to death as his dad thought was more his style? Would he really have been able to murder an innocent small child? Did he wait until I drove away to the phone box before letting himself quickly out of the house and running back to Don's house? And why did he come back a couple of hours later to sit in Mark Ward's kitchen? I wonder how many times a day any of us are that close to danger without ever realizing it? My churning imagination provided me with enough material for a hundred different nightmares.

The police also wondered if the original reason he took Julie's keys with him when he left was because he intended to return for the body in order to dispose of the evidence. Maybe, they suggested, he was planning to dissolve it in acid just as soon as he was able to get it out of the house. Or maybe he would have gone back and done it in the bathroom at Grange Avenue. But all that is no more than speculation because he never got a chance. If he had succeeded in disposing of Julie we might never have found out what happened to her. It would have been hard to have been left in the same state of limbo that we suffered for the first three months after her disappearance, but at the same time it would have left us with a tiny sliver of hope to cling to, a possibility that she had just walked away from her life in Billingham and started again in London or some other distant city.

For so much of that three-week trial Charlie and I were just sitting in the gallery staring down at Dunlop, focussing our hatred, watching his every move as the case went on around him, willing him to speak up and tell the truth. On the whole he seemed remarkably composed for a man who was on trial for murder, but we noticed he kept taking his slip-on shoes off, turning them round and trying to force his feet into them back to front. It was a strange nervous tic suggesting that there was something going on behind his otherwise immobile, silent and hostile façade even if the rest of us couldn't begin to guess what it was. Maybe a psychologist could explain that one.

His defence lawyer was good at his job, able to talk to the jury as though he was just holding a normal conversation with friends. He was much more convincing than the prosecuting counsel, who was posher and more from the old school. The prosecution man didn't seem to have much idea how to talk to ordinary people like the ones dozing on the jury benches. We noticed that when the defence counsel was talking to them they woke up and hung on his every word, nodding along to the points he was making, but we convinced ourselves it wouldn't matter in the long run because the evidence against Dunlop was so overwhelming. No matter what his defence counsel said, or how convincingly he said it, it was still completely obvious that Billy was the killer. He could give no plausible explanation why the keys were under his floorboards or why his semen was found on the blanket. He couldn't account for his movements during those hours between leaving the hospital and arriving home. He had a history of violence, particularly against women. It hardly seemed that we needed to go through the whole charade of a trial in order to find him guilty. So we assumed it didn't matter that a quarter of the jury was asleep and the defence lawyer was sounding so plausible; they were bound to find him guilty once the final question was asked, weren't they?

Towards the end of the three weeks Dunlop himself was put in the witness box and Charlie and I watched his every move like hawks, trying to work out what was going on inside his head, behind his expressionless face. He would shut his eyes, as if thinking deeply, before answering each question from the prosecuting barrister. It made him seem strangely sincere and believable, even though the things he was saying, like the fantasy about someone trying to frame him by putting his fingerprints on the key fob, made no sense at all. It was as if he truly believed the words he was speaking, as if he was honestly puzzled by how the whole misunderstanding could have come about.

'Somebody's trying to frame me for this,' he said again, his voice quiet and even and convincing. 'I didn't do it. I wouldn't. She was a lovely girl, really quiet.'

It sounded so sincere we almost felt like believing him ourselves at times, but the evidence was over-whelming, wasn't it? I began to wonder if it was me who was going mad. All the way through the trial, he stuck to his story that he knew nothing about what had hap-pened that night, insisting that someone was trying to frame him. He was in the witness box for almost a whole day as the prosecution lawyer kept battering away at him, trying to break him. The strain did seem to be get-ting to him and by the end of the afternoon he was shak-ing so violently that even his hair seemed to be trembling.

'You're losing your bottle, Mr Dunlop,' the prosecu-tor said, pressing his advantage, 'because you did kill this girl.'

Charlie and I were on the edges of our seats, certain that he was about to crack and confess. We were sure that if the prosecuting lawyer kept the pressure up with just a few more questions Dunlop wouldn't be able to hold out any longer and we would be certain to get the verdict we wanted so much to hear.

'You're shaking,' the lawyer kept on at him.

'No, I'm not,' Dunlop grunted. 'I didn't kill her.'

The shaking was getting worse and it looked as if he was about to give in and confess when the judge glanced up at the clock.

'It's quarter to four,' he said. 'We'll recess until tomorrow.'

I was bitterly disappointed as I watched Billy being escorted from the court, sure that if the prosecutor had been given another ten or fifteen minutes he would have been able to finish the job off once and for all. We had been so close and now we had to wait yet another day, and get through another long night of replaying the evidence in our heads over and over again.

By the next day Billy had rested and recovered his composure. The shaking had passed and he was back to sitting as still as a statue, but I felt confident we were going to get a conviction. Who was ever going to believe that anyone had been able to 'plant' his fingerprints on the key fob? The representatives of the Crown Prosecution Service I spoke to were equally confident, reassuring me whenever the doubts threatened to well up in me that all the evidence was in place and unarguable. The police were still totally convinced they were going to get their man. We felt we were nearly at the end of our long and arduous journey.

The trial came to an end and the jury was out for a whole day, deliberating on what their verdict should be.

Charlie and I sat waiting for news, barely daring to go to the toilet in case something happened. They were unable to come to a conclusion that day so they stayed in a hotel overnight and kept going the following day. It was hard to imagine what they could find to argue about, because it seemed so obvious what verdict they should return. They sent some pointless questions into the court via the usher that puzzled everyone, even the judge.

'I don't understand this jury,' he said at one point. 'Their questions don't seem to be about anything that is relevant to this trial.'

By the time they came back into the courtroom I could hardly breathe with the tension. What if something went wrong at this stage? What if the worst happened and they decided he wasn't guilty, that there was 'reasonable doubt'? Dunlop would immediately be back out on the streets and none of us would be safe.

'Can your foreman please stand?' Words I had heard hundreds of time in courtroom dramas were suddenly being spoken right in front of me.

At that moment there was a flurry of confusion and the jury realized they didn't have a foreman. No one had thought to elect one. A buzz went round the room as everyone wondered what this meant. It seemed that because they didn't have a foreman they weren't going to be able to reach a decision. I was finding it hard to take in what I was hearing. How was it possible that they had gone the whole three weeks without realizing they needed a foreman? Why hadn't anyone official told them what to do? What had they been talking about in that hotel room for the last two days? What was going to happen now? We soon found out.

Not only had they given no thought to electing a foreman, but it seemed that they had also been unable to reach a verdict, even on a majority basis. The judge ruled that he would have to discharge them from their duties and order a re-trial. He was obviously exasperated at the three weeks they had wasted, but his feelings didn't come close to the horror that we were feeling. This meant we were going to have to go through the whole nightmare again before we would hear Dunlop being found guilty of murder, and I truly didn't know if I would be able to find the strength to endure the ordeal. It felt as though every ounce of energy I possessed had been used to get me through this first trial. How would I survive another?

Chapter Fourteen

Reliving the Nightmare

The re-trial of Billy Dunlop didn't take place
until October 1991, so we had to endure six
more months of living in limbo, not knowing what the
future held for us. After the fiasco of the first trial my
confidence had been shaken. I had been told by the
police that they were '110 per cent' certain of a conviction and they were still just as sure that their case was
watertight as they had been before the initial trial. But
now I realized that however strong the evidence, you
couldn't be sure of anything when it came to dealing
with the legal system. No one could predict what the
intelligence of the jury would be like. If they simply
didn't understand what was being said, or allowed Billy's confident lies or the defence barrister's easy elo-
quence to convince them, then all the police's
certainties were worth nothing. It was like being with

Lewis Carroll's *Alice in Wonderland*, in a place where good sense and logic didn't necessarily mean a thing, and where anything might happen, however mad, impossible or contradictory it might seem. It is hard to think straight when nothing makes sense and all the things you once took for granted are shown to be something different.

My family's lives had been totally changed by one inexplicable act of violence that hit us out of the blue. Then a trial that had seemed like little more than a formality had turned into a fiasco. I would never again believe that you could be sure about anything. I had learned the hard way that there are no certainties in life and nothing can be taken for granted. I had always taken it for granted that I would outlive my children, and I had taken it for granted that Billy Dunlop would be found guilty at the first trial. Things kept on upsetting the balance of what seemed right and predictable.

Between the two trials I bumped into Jayne, the mother of Dunlop's two boys, coming out of the health centre. It was a strangely mundane setting in which to meet someone I had previously seen in the pressured surrounds of the trial.

'How are you doing?' she asked when she spotted me. It sounded as though she genuinely cared and wanted to know the answer.

'I'm all right,' I replied cautiously, not wanting to

open up too much, still not quite sure what to expect from her.

'I hope they get him next time,' she said, 'because if they don't it'll be me he'll kill next.'

Her words shocked me, reminding me just how important it was to other people that Dunlop was convicted as well as to us. The police had told me how dangerous they believed he was, and now I was hearing the same from the woman who probably knew him better than anyone. Sometimes I worried that I was becoming obsessed with keeping him off the streets because of what he had done to Julie, and that it might only be because I wanted revenge for Julie's death. But when I heard Jayne saying she feared for her own life I knew for certain that our cause was just. Dunlop was a danger to society as a whole, not just to our family, and he couldn't be allowed to get away with this murder and come back out to terrorize and kill again. I tried to convince myself that although the first trial had turned out to be a joke, it was just a freak occurrence. The re-trial was bound to see him put away for a long time. Wasn't it?

This time the case was being heard by Judge Harry Ognall, who had presided over many high-profile murder trials before, including that of the notorious Peter Sutcliffe, known in the media as 'The Yorkshire Ripper'. That news was encouraging, making me feel as though we were going to be in safe, experienced hands.

Charlie and I then had the nightmare of having to sit through the entire trial again from start to finish, so that a new jury and judge could completely understand all the evidence and all the arguments. We were being forced to experience some of the worst weeks of our lives all over again, like some sort of torture specially designed to drive us insane. We had to hear all the medical details gathered from Julie's poor abandoned body, and all the details of her sexual flings in the last few months of her short life. As the days passed and the voices below us droned on, I spent a lot of hours staring at the jury, trying to work out what they were thinking and whether they were going to be more intelligent than the last lot, desperately trying to convince myself that things were going to turn out all right this time. During the days we would be sitting in court, and during the nights, when I had finally calmed down enough to climb into bed, all the arguments and facts and worries would be going round and round in my wakeful head as I waited for the moment when I would have to get up and start another day's ordeal.

Once more the judge sent the jury out at the end of the trial to deliberate on everything they had heard and to decide if Billy Dunlop was guilty of the crime he was accused of. During the whole second trial we hadn't heard a single new piece of evidence or any new theories that had changed our minds in the slightest as to

Dunlop's guilt. All we had to do, surely, was wait for the jury to announce the obvious conclusion.

The police allowed Charlie and me to come down from the public gallery into the body of the courtroom and there we sat for one agonizing hour after another, waiting to hear a result that would make all the difference to our lives and take a dangerous killer off the streets of Billingham.

'It's not looking too promising,' one of the detectives, Detective Inspector Dave Scott, told us quietly and for a moment I thought I must have heard him wrong.

'What do you mean?' I was shocked. I couldn't believe that even the police were now losing faith in getting the verdict they felt assured of. How could they be talking like this now when they had been so confident of a conviction at the beginning of the first trial?

'If this jury are unable to reach a verdict, it's possible that the judge will acquit Dunlop,' he said.

'But what about all the evidence against him?' I asked, aghast.

He shrugged his shoulders. 'That's what could happen.'

I couldn't make his words sink into my brain past all the exhaustion and all the medication. I just couldn't understand what he was saying. The thought that Dunlop might walk free after we had been through so much was too terrible even to contemplate.

A few minutes later, after five hours of waiting, Judge Ognall called the jurors back into the court.

'Have you reached a unanimous verdict?' he asked.

'No,' came the reply.

He asked if they could agree on a majority verdict, but the answer was still no. So the judge acquitted Billy Dunlop, just as the police had come to fear he would. Just like that, it was all over and Billy Dunlop was going to be able to walk from the court a free man.

It took a few moments for his words to sink in and then I leapt to my feet. I felt a wave of hysteria rising up inside me, threatening to sweep away what was left of my sanity. I couldn't stop myself from screaming out at the top of my voice all the thoughts that were crowding into my brain.

'He killed our daughter and he's walking free!' I yelled. 'What's going to happen now?'

As I grappled to get my thoughts together and work out what had gone wrong I remembered that the reason the pathologist had been unable to confirm whether Julie had been strangled or asphyxiated was because of the condition of her body. If the police had found her within the first few days of her death we might have had a very different outcome.

'The police should have found her!' I screamed.

All my anger and my fears and my grief poured out, the rush of emotion too much for my legs to be able to cope with as they buckled beneath me and I found myself on the floor of the courtroom, still screaming and thrashing helplessly around, unable to believe that after a year of suffering our nightmare had just become even worse. Mark Braithwaite had accompanied us that day and he had to lift me up off the floor and help me from the courtroom, trying to console me as we went, because Charlie was caught up in his own state of acute shock. I remember I was punching Mark as he pulled me from the room.

'What happens now?' I kept crying. 'What happens now?'

I felt as though I was the one who had been given the life sentence; one that I would be serving in purgatory. After all we had been through we were now going to have to go home knowing that Billy Dunlop was living up the road and would be as free to come knocking on our door as we were to knock on his.

I was so confused. None of it made sense. I couldn't understand what had happened. How could the whole weight of the police force be on our side and still not be able to get Billy locked up for a crime he had obviously committed? Dazed with shock and disbelief, I was like a small child lost in a grown-up world. I kept on asking people to explain it to me, but nobody could. No one involved in the case could understand why the jury could have been left in any doubt that Billy had killed

Julie that night, nor could they understand why the judge was willing to allow Billy back out onto the street after listening to all the evidence of how evil and violent he was.

The only thing that the jury didn't have was a confirmed cause of death, which our solicitor told us would probably have gone a long way to helping them make up their minds. But what did it matter whether Julie was strangled or asphyxiated? They had a dead girl who the pathologist had confirmed had come to a violent end, and they had the man who had done it to her. It was the simplest thing in the world to piece it all together, wasn't it?

Somehow the prosecution barrister hadn't been able to paint in that final detail of the actual moment of death vividly enough for the jury, leaving just an element of doubt hovering in the air, and while that doubt hovered they couldn't bring themselves to convict him.

Billy Dunlop had got away with murdering our child and was going to be back out on the streets of Billingham, free to kill again. The police were equally stunned, having believed that they had been about to put one of the most dangerous men in the area behind bars for life. Now they had an hysterical woman on their hands as well, who was leaving them in no doubt that she blamed them for everything that had gone wrong.

Eventually they managed to coax me into a car and drove me home, sobbing uncontrollably, unable to imagine how I was going to cope with the years that now stretched ahead of us with no Julie, no justice and no way of feeling that anything had ended. By the time we were sitting indoors I was drained of strength and we all just sat in a devastated silence as we tried to get our heads round what had happened.

The next day there were big pictures in the papers showing him back with Jayne and his boys, and she was saying she would stand by him and that she had always known he was innocent. I suppose she had to say that for fear of what he would do to her if she didn't, but at the time I felt she had betrayed me too. I told myself that she must have been lying when she told me she wanted him put away. I felt we had been entirely defeated and Julie's life had been shown to be worth nothing to anyone but us.

The following afternoon Billy gave an interview on Tyne Tees Television. He complained to the interviewer that he had been wrongfully locked up for twenty months and now he wanted the police to reopen the case in order to point the finger at the right man. He also said he thought he should receive compensation for what the police had put him through as an innocent man. He sounded strangely convincing but we still didn't believe a single bit of it.

With those few words from the judge and the jury Billy Dunlop had gone from being a murder suspect, facing a sentence of at least twelve years, to a free man who could claim he had been wrongfully accused and imprisoned. He could go home to his woman and his children, or down the pub or the rugby club, and there was nothing anyone could do to stop him. He was free to go back to being part of the 'Crazy Gang', abusing women and starting fights, and that was exactly what he did.

If he had a reputation in the area for being a frightening man before the trial, he had even more power to intimidate and bully now, because he was the man who had proved he could kill and walk away, scot-free. He had shown that he was above the law and that no one could touch him.

Once I had recovered from the shock of him being let off, I decided that I was never going to give up hope of getting him back in front of another judge. He might be feeling cocky today, I thought, but he was reckoning without the determination of a couple of parents who were intent on getting justice for their child.

I was terrified to go into Billingham, even to the town centre during the middle of the day when it would be crowded with shoppers, for fear of bumping into him. I didn't want to risk losing control in front of him. In all the documentaries I made and television interviews

I gave over the years, I made sure I wasn't filmed getting upset because I knew he would be watching them eventually and I didn't want him to think I was losing my self-control. I wanted him to know that Charlie and I were not giving up, that we were still on his trail. It was a personal vendetta between him and us, a war of nerves. Sometimes it was hard not to get emotional but I was determined to remain focussed until I had achieved my goal of getting him found guilty and punished for the murder. I was afraid that if I bumped into him in the street I would lose it and start screaming and ranting, maybe even attacking him, and then he would know that he had truly destroyed us.

The police must have realized how strongly we felt about him. When he was first acquitted and released they came to see us and warned Charlie and Gary to stay away from him, fearing that if they did anything to Dunlop they might get hurt themselves, and it could spoil the police's chances of getting him for something else later. They were pretty sure he'd step out of line again before too long and hoped to be able to put him safely behind bars when that happened.

I know how much Charlie and Gary must have wanted to do something to avenge Julie's death, because I felt the same way. I would actually drive around in the car sometimes, hoping I would see him crossing the road so that I could run him over. I didn't care what happened to me as long as I got some justice for Julie. I could actually visualize myself knocking him down and then driving back and forwards over him until I squashed him flat. I'm told that is typical behaviour for someone suffering from post-traumatic stress disorder. I have no idea if I would actually have done it had the opportunity arisen but I certainly believed I wanted to.

The only one of us who did come face to face with him was Angela, Julie's sister. As she walked past him in the street he looked up, saw her and turned to walk away, leaving her standing there, shaking with a mixture of shock, anger and fear. She was still shaking from head to foot when she told me about it later. Poor Angela. Her reaction to this, as it was to the murder itself, was to shut it all inside. She still can't talk about her feelings about it very well. Maybe I would have been struck down in the same way if it had been me who met Dunlop in the street; I just don't know.

Martin, my therapist, said that I had to force myself to start going into town in order to get over my fears, just as I had forced myself to go back into that bathroom.

'Begin by going round the perimeter of the town first,' he said, 'then go quickly in and out, staying a little longer each time.'

I did everything he advised me because I did want to get over my fears. I didn't want Dunlop dictating where I could and couldn't go for the rest of my life. I didn't want him having any control over my life. All the time I was in town I was looking around, trying to spot him, not wanting to come across him unexpectedly as Angela had.

Some while later, I got a phone call from a friend of mine who lived near Billy to say that she'd seen him drinking in a pub in town.

'Ann, you're not going to believe this but he was a bit drunk and I heard him boasting to anyone who would listen about how he had got away with killing Julie; how he had pulled off the perfect murder.'

I felt a rush of shock and sheer rage so fierce that I nearly collapsed on the spot. I called Charlie through and repeated what I'd heard. He went white with fury. 'If I tell the police, will you testify to this?' I asked, and my friend said she would. I hung up and rang Mark Braithwaite straight away to let him know.

'I think you'd better come and see me,' he said.

A few more friends I spoke to corroborated the story that Billy was gloating about getting away with murder. It made me even angrier and even more afraid of what he might do to us if he got a chance. But at the same time I felt a chink of hope; if he was openly boasting about what he had done, surely that would give the police another chance to arrest him? This was a confession, wasn't it? Just because he had got away with it in front of one judge didn't mean he would get away with it again, especially if there were people who would testify that he was openly confessing.

When we went to see Mark Braithwaite to discuss this with him, it turned out that he had also heard the rumours of Dunlop's alleged boasting. 'But there's nothing we can do about it because of the law on double jeopardy.'

'What does that mean?' I asked.

'Because he's been acquitted formally by a judge he can't be tried again for murder. That's the law. It's been that way for hundreds of years'.

This was news to me. Surely if someone was admitting to something the police should arrest and seek to put them on trial again? But apparently that was not possible, and never had been for as long as there had been widespread law and order in England. In the eighteenth century one juror described the law as meaning, 'no man shall be brought into jeopardy of his life and limb more than once for the same offence.'

As I tried to take in the full meaning of this, it felt as though Dunlop was actually laughing at us. Charlie had vowed to Julie that he would get the man who killed her, and now we were being told that that could never be the case because he had been acquitted and therefore couldn't be tried again. Every fibre of my body screamed out that I should pursue Dunlop until I finally got him put behind bars, but now I was being told that the law was going to be on his side, not mine.

It had been suggested to us previously that we could consider taking out a private prosecution against him, where the burden of proof is not as great as that in criminal trials. He might well be found guilty in a civil court but he couldn't be jailed as a result, so it wouldn't achieve the one thing we wanted, which was to get Billy Dunlop behind bars. Also, we wouldn't get legal aid to pursue a private prosecution and would have to pay thousands out of our own pockets. I would have considered this money well spent if it got Dunlop a life sentence but seemingly all it would mean would be that we could claim compensation from him for damages. And no money could ever compensate us for what he'd done.

I couldn't believe what I was hearing. I was Alice in Wonderland again, thrown into a world where nothing made sense and everything was the opposite of how it should be. How could it be possible that this man was openly admitting he'd killed Julie but he couldn't be arrested for it because of some ancient law? It seemed like just one more slap in the face for us and for Julie's memory. We went away from our meeting with Mark feeling as helpless as the police did. Was there nothing we could do to stop this man? No way we could bring him to justice?

Well-meaning people kept telling me that I had to just accept what had happened and hope that Billy would be caught for something else later on. I could see that for the sake of my own sanity they were right. But I just couldn't accept it. How could I do that to Julie? How could I give up on my fight for justice for my daughter? How would I feel if I turned a blind eye and he killed someone else's daughter? It wasn't possible to let it go. There had to be something we could do, if I could just work out what it was.

After Billy was released, the inquest into Julie's death was resumed. That evening as Charlie and I sat at home together, he began to feel very unwell. His face was pale and he was complaining of tightness in his chest, so I called an ambulance and he was taken to hospital where they told us he had suffered a minor heart attack. It was yet one more way in which Dunlop had injured my family. After that, we decided that Charlie should stop running his catering trailer and take things easier. I'd lost one person I loved with all my heart and there was no way I was going to risk losing another.

Chapter Fifteen

Whispers and Rumours

Although my relationship with Mark Braithwaite and other individual members of the murder investigation team was good, my anger at the initial mess the police had made of finding Julie's body did not lessen with time. I still blamed them for the fact that the jury had let Dunlop off. If they had listened to me the first time I told them she was missing, and if they had searched the house properly, they would have found her body and the evidence would probably still have been fresh enough for any jury to convict Billy – even one that was half asleep.

Once I'd had time to find out more about the law of double jeopardy, I still couldn't see that it was right for it to apply to our situation. Its defenders claimed it provided an essential limit on the power of the state. They said there was a danger that if a court came to an unpopular decision when they acquitted someone, the police or the newspapers could force them to keep trying and re-trying the same person, persecuting them forever for something that they had been acquitted of fairly and squarely at the beginning. But I couldn't see how that could apply to someone who was openly boasting to the whole world about a murder he had committed.

I could understand it wasn't fair to keep on re-trying someone unless there was an incredibly good reason for doing so, but I felt that Billy Dunlop mouthing off to anyone who would listen about how he had pulled off the perfect crime was about as good a reason for a re-trial as it was possible to have. I was aware, of course, that it could seem that I only thought that way because I was personally involved, but there was nothing I could do about that. When your daughter has been murdered everything becomes personal, but that doesn't make your point of view any less valid.

Once I'd had time to recover a little from the shock of the trial, I decided that there was no way I was going to let this setback stop me from finding a way of getting Dunlop put behind bars to serve a life sentence. There now seemed to be two possible options open to me: one was to campaign to get the law changed, and the other was to hope the police would arrest Dunlop for something else that he could be given a life sentence for. The former would be the most satisfactory outcome, but the latter might be the easier result to achieve. The idea that people like us could actually get the law of the land changed seemed an impossible dream, but I certainly wasn't going to rule it out as a possibility. I've always believed you can achieve anything if you just put your mind to it and keep on going, but I wasn't quite sure how you set about changing an actual law.

Rather than wait for Billy to commit another crime, and condemn another family to the same purgatory we were going through, we decided it would be better to try to get him tried for something else he had already done. There were plenty of rumours circulating about other crimes that people in the area generally believed Billy Dunlop was responsible for – in fact we were quite spoiled for choice. Often he didn't even seem to try very hard to cover his tracks, almost as if he felt himself to be invincible and above the law, which he had now pretty much proved himself to be by getting away with killing Julie.

The more we thought about it, the more incredible we found it that such a potentially dangerous man could be allowed to walk the streets when so much was known about his propensity to extreme violence.

Over the following years we heard any number of different whispers and rumours from police officers we met, or from journalists and television reporters who had all been delving for clues in different places, talking to different sources at different times and coming to different conclusions. It was always hard to tell what was myth and what was likely to be true, but whatever we heard never made us doubt for a moment that Billy Dunlop had killed our Julie.

I was constantly nagging for the police to get him arrested and taken off the streets again as quickly as possible before he had time to kill anyone else. I didn't want any other family to have to go through what we had all been through. Aware that I had no real influence over anyone in the police force beyond my ability to be a permanent nuisance to them, I needed to find other people who would be willing to speak up on our behalf in the campaign to get Dunlop back behind bars. I went to visit our MP, a man called Frank Cook, to ask if he could do anything to influence the police to pay more attention to what we were saying.

To be honest I'd never had much of an opinion of politicians up till then, always thinking they were all talk and no action, but Frank Cook was brilliant right from the start. He understood exactly what I was trying to achieve and why it was important, and agreed to give us his support in any way possible. I always found that if I was able to talk face-to-face to anyone long enough to explain my case, they always agreed with me that something needed to be done. Now we would have to wait to see if he was all talk or whether he would actually help us. As it turned out, he was one of the first people we came across who was actually willing to put his influence where his mouth was.

Good as his word, he started by getting in touch with the new Deputy Chief Constable and asking him to talk to us. The man agreed immediately and arranged to come to my house with another high-ranking officer – maybe they'd heard my reputation for attacking officers over the chest freezer and felt safer travelling in pairs. It's amazing what a different result you get when it's an MP asking for something to happen rather than just a normal member of the public like me. The other officer even rang up before they arrived to tell us they would be with us in about an hour, and saying his boss had asked him to check we didn't mind him turning up in his uniform.

'I don't care if he comes in the Full Monty,' I said, 'as long as he comes.'

'Get that central heating stoked up,' I told Charlie as soon as I was off the phone. 'I'll get that uniform off him.'

By the time they arrived, Charlie had got the house steaming like a sauna, but the Deputy Chief Constable still never undid so much as a button of his jacket. The poor man sat there, bright red in the face and sweating like a pig, trying to explain rationally to us how the police were doing their best to take Dunlop off the streets. I had to admire him for having the bottle to come and see us in person, away from the safety of his own office – something his predecessor had never done – but I wasn't convinced they were anywhere close to succeeding.

Over successive years I noticed that things did improve a great deal in the way the police force dealt with the public in general and with victims' families in particular. The notorious Stephen Lawrence case definitely had an influence on this. Stephen Lawrence was a young black lad who was murdered at a bus stop in South London in 1993 by a violent gang of white racist thugs. The police made such a mess of the investigation that the perpetrators got away with it, despite reports that they were swaggering around and boasting that they had done it. After an official investigation it was admitted that there was 'institutional racism' within the police force that had contributed to things going so badly wrong for the prosecution. The MacPherson Report into the case made a number of recommendations about ways murder cases should be handled differently in future. It was as if the police realized they couldn't patronize the general public any more, that they had to acknowledge we were intelligent, feeling human beings, just like themselves, not statistics to be processed, and that they needed to communicate with us accordingly.

The new Chief Constable for our area actually started holding 'police meetings' in local halls, where a few high-ranking officers faced the public from time to time and listened to any issues or questions they had. Charlie and I went to one and sat ourselves down in the front row, right beneath the podium. We stayed quiet for a while, letting everyone else ask their questions, getting the measure of the event. When one of the officers enquired if there were any more questions before they wound up the proceedings, I raised my hand in the air.

'I have a question for the Chief Constable,' I said. 'There's a murderer walking the streets of Billingham. I just wondered when you are going to get him off the streets before he murders someone else?'

A deathly silence fell over the room as everyone waited to hear the answer.

'Can I firstly say how much I admire your courage for coming?' the same officer said, almost seeming to choke on his own words.

'I don't wish to appear rude,' I persevered, 'but I have directed my question to the Chief Constable, if you wouldn't mind letting him speak.'

'I don't know the case you are referring to,' the Chief Constable said, realizing his colleague wasn't going to be able to get him off the hook, 'because I wasn't in the job then.'

'No,' I said, 'I understand that. And I admire your courage for coming here too, but I would like an answer to my question.'

'I think,' he said, 'on that note we'll close the meeting.'

That was the end of that interaction with the public, and someone from lower down the ranks was sent out to talk to us again a few days later. It seemed there was a limit to how open and communicative they were willing to be with the public, whatever impression their public relations division wanted to give. I realized the police must be getting fed up with hearing from me by then, wanting the whole thing to settle down and disappear, but I didn't care. I wasn't going to stop making a nuisance of myself until I had found a way of getting Billy Dunlop off the streets and convicted of Julie's murder.

After he was acquitted there were people who started to wonder whether he had been the culprit after all. There were some who were beginning to think that we might be persecuting an innocent man, blinded by our grief and unwilling to accept that we had been proved wrong in court. If you hadn't actually been in the courtroom and heard all the evidence for yourself, you could have been forgiven for assuming that the judge and jury got it right and that the wrong man had been fingered for the crime. But as a family, having followed every twist and turn of the case from the start, we never wavered for even a moment in our belief that we had the right man in our sights, and nor did any of the police who we were in touch with. Having listened to the trial twice over, and having heard all the evidence, we were completely convinced Dunlop had killed Julie, even before he started boasting about it. But we felt completely helpless to do anything to put things right and Billy seemed to be rubbing our faces in it. It was as though he thought he was invincible. His arrogance only strengthened our determination to find a way to bring him to justice.

Our private campaign (which I dare say seemed more like a vendetta from Billy Dunlop's side of the fence) probably helped to keep me sane during the following years. I needed something to focus on, something to take my mind off the flashbacks and the anger that was constantly seething inside me. I couldn't just accept that it was all over and Dunlop was acquitted; I had to keep thinking of how I could change things. It gave me something to hope for and dream about at moments when otherwise everything would have seemed totally bleak and hopeless.

Once I got my head round the idea that it had actually happened and Julie truly had gone from us, I just kept on thinking about how I could find another way to get Dunlop convicted and it gave me a positive channel for everything bad that had occurred since that November night in 1989. If we could succeed in taking Billy Dunlop off the street then Julie's death would not have been completely meaningless; some good would have come from it.

Chapter Sixteen

Living with the consequences

After a year of living separately, Charlie and I decided it was stupid for us both to be paying rent and that we should try to be together again. I wanted to take care of him if I could, especially after he had his heart attack. We still had the money from selling the bungalow in Billingham just before Julie died, so we bought ourselves another bungalow in Norton, a village a few miles away, and tried to find a way to get through the long days and nights together as we continued to wait for an opportunity to get back on Dunlop's trail.

Living in the bungalow was harder than we had imagined it would be. As long as Billy Dunlop was on the loose we felt in danger of being attacked by him. It is hard to get to sleep in your bed at night when you know there is someone out there who is capable of doing such terrible things, who doesn't seem to care who he hurts or kills, and who knows where you live. Every passing noise triggers your imagination as you lie there picturing the worst. I was determined not to allow my nervousness to stop me from pursuing my campaign to have him imprisoned for Julie's murder, but that didn't make the fears any the less, particularly in the small hours of the morning when your brain plays tricks on you anyway. I knew that you had to stand up to bullies or they would never leave you alone, but I was still afraid of him.

The nightmare of knowing he was out there and could come looking for us at any time continued for nearly two years and eventually we realized it wasn't a strain worth putting up with and moved again to a flat in a big block in Norton, feeling we would be more secure there. We hoped we would be more protected by being on a high floor, surrounded on all sides by kind neighbours.

At the same time as I was learning more and more about the murky underworld that men like Billy Dunlop inhabited in my own home town, I was also learning a lot about what was going on in the darkness inside my own head. My counsellor, Martin, was a huge help in making me understand how the symptoms of post-traumatic stress disorder (PSTD) manifested themselves. I worked with him for over three years after finding Julie's body and, while the pain and the unhappiness hadn't really got any better, I decided to stop going to see him after that, as I felt ready to try fighting my demons on my own.

In 1994, I watched a documentary on television about a hospital in East Sussex called Ticehurst and I realized that I was by no means the only person to suffer from PTSD. The documentary featured Gordon Turnbull, a consultant psychiatrist working at Ticehurst who had been in the RAF and had become a specialist in PTSD. Several Middle Eastern hostages went to this hospital when they were released from captivity and needed to sort out their emotions in order to readjust to normal life. As I watched the stories of four different patients during the documentary, I realized that their symptoms were very similar to mine. One of them was a girl who had found her parents' murdered bodies. Just like me, she was suffering from intrusive thoughts and an inability to concentrate and Gordon Turnbull seemed to know exactly how to help her.

At the end of the programme I sat down and wrote to him, telling him what had happened to me. He wrote back a lovely letter, saying he thought he could help me. I went for an assessment and my GP helped me to get funding to go to Ticehurst as an in-patient. It was a turning point for me.

I was part of a group of five patients with similar symptoms and we all went together into an intense, deep therapy. Gordon Turnbull was wonderful. One of the other patients was a very arrogant and bombastic police officer. Initially he was the last person I thought I needed to be exposed to given my hostility towards the police, but he and I were actually really good for one another, both of us helping the other to appreciate that there are two sides to every story. When you are as filled with grief and shock and anger as I had been it is hard to appreciate that there might be any other side to anything. Everything had been very black and white in my world ever since the day Julie vanished but this encounter helped me to appreciate that there might be some shades of grey in between.

Ticehurst is a beautiful, great big old house set in its own tranquil grounds and we lived together in the lodge house to the main building. Just to be away from the area surrounding Billingham was a relief, a chance to breathe different air and get some perspective on where our lives were going. It was hard to move forward when everything I did or saw reminded me of Julie. If I went into a shop, walked down a familiar street or looked at a view, I could remember doing the same with her in the past. In East Sussex I was free of all those reminders.

I saw a video designed to help patients with their therapy. It talked about flashbacks and this rang a lot of bells for me. A year or so earlier I had been in a bathroom showroom with Charlie and I came across a bath where they had taken the side off in order to show all the workings underneath. Charlie was walking in front of me and all he heard was me shouting. As he turned round he was just in time to see me running from the shop as hysterically as I ran down the stairs at Grange Avenue after finding Julie, frantically trying to escape all over again from the phantom smells invading my nostrils and the sights I was seeing in my head.

Being in Ticehurst helped me to accept that the flashbacks were a normal reaction to an abnormal situation. Until then I had been terrified of them, just as I might have been of a terrible physical pain. I was an inpatient there for two weeks, and then I went back for a visit every three months for the following year, and I can't speak too highly of the staff there. I told them things I have never told anyone else in my life. You're frightened that if you talk about some things you'll transfer your pain to someone else. There's a song that goes 'Sometimes when we touch, the honesty's too much' and I think it could have been written about post-traumatic stress disorder, because that's exactly what it feels like. But with the Ticehurst staff and in group therapy sessions with the other patients, I was able to talk about my intrusive thoughts and I learned that they are normal. Before going there, there had been times when I thought I was actually going mad, but they taught me I wasn't. I was a sane human being in horrific circumstances, just getting by as best I could.

211

Chapter Seventeen

Billy Runs Amok

We had heard from other people that Billy was still acting violently towards his girlfriend, Jayne, and one day we were told she decided she'd put up with all she could take. She finally plucked up the courage to go to the police to tell them he had threatened to kill her. Knowing what Billy was capable of the police listened to her sympathetically and took her fears seriously. At this time, Jayne had moved to a safe house near Manchester, but Billy tracked her down. He came across a phone number on the phone of a friend of Jayne's and sat going through phone directories in the local library until he could put an address to it. One day he went to look for her.

So confident was he of his untouchability, he even went into a police station to ask for directions to the address where she was hiding out. It was almost as though he was daring them to try to stop him, showing them that he was out of their reach and above the law, that he could go wherever he wanted and do whatever he chose. The police were already on to him after threats he had made, and he was recognized at the station. He was arrested and charged with threatening to kill Jayne, and in January 1997 he received a short custodial sentence of a few months. Charlie and I went to court and watched from the public gallery as he was convicted.

It was nice to have him behind bars for a bit, and we slept much easier while he was inside, but it didn't change things in the long term. I still had to learn to cope in a world where people like him walked the streets and got away with unspeakable evil.

When Dunlop was released from jail he returned to Billingham and took up with a new girl called Donna, who lived in a block of flats near to his. I don't know what happened between them but I guess there was some sort of row because it wasn't long before he badly assaulted her and another man, a friend of hers called Shaun Fairweather.

He attacked Shaun violently, breaking several bones in his face and knocking him unconscious in the process. Next he turned on Donna and stabbed her with an oven fork, puncturing her lung. Had her brother and friends not arrived at that moment Dunlop would almost certainly have kept beating and stabbing them without so much as a thought for the consequences.

On this occasion his assaults had taken place in front of witnesses and both his victims were still alive to explain exactly what had happened, so we thought there was no chance of him getting away with it. He was arrested and charged with attempted murder.

This all happened over a bank holiday weekend when Charlie and I had taken Kevin to Scarborough for a break, so we didn't hear anything about it. I came back home on the Monday, although Charlie and Kevin were staying on for the rest of the week, because I was due to go to work the following day. I was still blissfully unaware of what had been going on as I let myself in through the front door. As I picked up the Saturday evening newspaper, which was lying on the mat, I immediately noticed the headline: 'Billingham man charged with attempted murder of two people.'

Just as I sat down and started to read the article, the phone rang.

'Where have you been?' Mark Braithwaite wanted to know the moment I picked the phone up. 'I thought you might be interested to know that Billy Dunlop has been arrested and charged with the attempted murder of two people over the weekend.'

I realized he was talking about the story that I had just that moment been reading. The 'Billingham man' was Billy Dunlop and I felt a rush of different emotions all at once; there was horror for the two victims, anger that Dunlop had been allowed to stay free long enough to ruin yet more lives and a mixture of excitement and relief at the thought that he must finally have pushed his luck too far and that this time he wouldn't be able to escape the consequences of his actions.

A few days later, once the swelling on his face had subsided, Shaun Fairweather went in for surgery. Despite everything I had seen over the years I was still shocked to see the extent of the damage that Billy had caused in those few frenzied minutes. You wouldn't have recognized Shaun as being human when they wheeled him in on a trolley; his face was completely pulverized. It made me shudder to think that the legal system had allowed a man who was capable of doing something like this out onto the streets when they had had the chance to lock him up for good. It was like letting a savage dog loose without a muzzle in a children's playground.

It definitely looked as if Dunlop would have difficulty escaping from this charge, but then it had looked that way when he stood trial for Julie's killing, so I wasn't going to count my chickens until I was completely sure they'd well and truly hatched.

We went to Billy's court appearance, just as we'd been to all the others, haunting his every step, wanting to know every detail in case something came up that would give us a chance to pin Julie's murder on him. Sometimes on these occasions Charlie and I would be the only ones sitting in the public gallery, like Pinky and Perky, inseparable and determined to see it through. I was always bristling with anger, while Charlie was silent and inscrutable. We must have driven Dunlop mad, like a couple of tireless avenging angels.

One day during the trial the police had trouble getting him to come out of his cell and into the courtroom and he told the detective in charge that he was frightened of Charlie. Maybe he'd watched too many late-night martial arts and Triad gangster films in his time – who knows? He must have thought we would never go away, like that sheriff and his posse who chased Butch Cassidy and the Sundance Kid wherever they went, always there in the distance, sending up a cloud of dust that the outlaws could see on the horizon whenever they turned round or stopped to rest. Seeing Charlie's impassive face across the visiting room in Durham back in 1990, and then in every courtroom he had ever appeared in since then, must have been getting to Dunlop; he must have wondered if we would ever give up. We could have told him the answer to that question – never!

To start with he was charged with the attempted murder of both victims, but he offered pleas of guilty to two counts of wounding with intent to cause grievous bodily harm. The court accepted his pleas even though the judge knew Billy's history. Despite almost killing two people in front of witnesses he was sentenced to just seven years in prison.

Donna, the girl he had stabbed, was watching from the public gallery just near us and the two of them started shouting up and down to one another. He asked her to come and visit him inside, and she agreed.

'Are you stupid?' Charlie asked her bluntly.

'He's already killed our daughter and he's tried to kill you,' I said, 'and you intend to go visiting him?'

She went quiet after that; maybe she was just too frightened of him to refuse anything he asked for, in the same way that Jayne had been too frightened not to take him back after he was acquitted.

While it was a relief to know that he was finally off the street, seven years did not seem an adequate punishment for what he had done to Shaun and Donna, let alone what he had done to Julie. The chances were he would be out again before the end of his sentence anyway. It felt as though he was still mocking the system, and us, showing us that he could get away with murder, letting us know that sooner or later he would be back in Billingham to taunt us.

Even once he was inside he still seemed to believe he was invincible. It is my understanding that he sent a threatening letter to Donna, describing what he would do to her when he was released.

Terrified, Donna, who just a few months before had been willing to go and visit him in prison, took the letter to the police. They added it to the file of evidence they were building up against him, but it made no difference because he still couldn't be retried for murder as long as the law of double jeopardy remained the same.

What I didn't realize, however, was that whilst in prison, Dunlop had befriended a woman prison officer. The two of them would talk casually together for hours when they met around the prison and the police saw another opportunity to tempt him to incriminate himself. With the support of the prison service authorities, they wired up the officer to record all her conversations with Dunlop. I think they were keen to do whatever they could to make up to us for their previous mistakes, and we appreciated that.

After weeks of patient work the prison officer had recorded a staggering sixty hours of tape, during which Dunlop openly talked about killing Julie, crowing about how there was nothing anyone could do about it now because of the law relating to double jeopardy. With the tapes in their possession the police weren't going to have to rely on hearsay, such as people saying they had heard him confessing in a pub somewhere, if they ever managed to get him back into court. If the law could ever be changed and he could be put back on trial they wanted to be ready for him. The tapes were filed along with the letter to Donna as they prepared to spring their trap.

When they felt ready to pounce two officers, Peter Wilson and Dave Duffy, came to tell us what their new plan was. They explained that they now had him confessing on tape and that although he couldn't be retried for the murder, they could charge him with perjury. Perjury means lying when you are under oath in court. Dunlop had given evidence at both his trials for Julie's murder and had denied any involvement. It was a serious charge, even if it still wasn't the one we wanted him to have to face. The maximum sentence for perjury was seven years, which would be a lot better than nothing.

'Surely to goodness,' I said to Charlie once the police had gone, 'they'll give him the maximum. If he serves seven years for each of the times he lied in court that will make fourteen years in all. That would be a good result for us because if he'd been convicted for killing Julie in 1991 the tariff for murder then was only twelve years, so at least he'll be behind bars for a decent length of time, even if we can't make it for murdering our Julie.'

I don't know at what stage Billy realized that he had opened himself up to being prosecuted for perjury; probably it wasn't until his solicitor informed him that he was being charged. I imagine he was pretty angry with himself for slipping up so badly when he found out. It was a stupid mistake to make just in order to give himself the chance to brag and act like a hard man around the prison. When he realized the police had everything on tape, Billy agreed to give them a formal confession. Maybe he thought they would go easier on him if it looked as though he was finally co-operating.

At last we were going to learn a few more facts about what had happened that night, even if it was only his version and we still couldn't be sure he was telling the whole truth.

In his confession he told the police that after coming out of the hospital on the night of the violence at the rugby club strip show, having had his eyebrow stitched, he had gone to look for Mark Ward at Kath's house in Grange Avenue to tell him what had happened. According to Billy's story, Mark had already gone to bed when he reached the house, but Billy noticed that Julie's lights were still on next door, as she had only just been dropped back from her pizza delivery round by the Iranian. He said he'd decided to knock on her door and that she'd let him in and made him a cup of tea. They sat chatting for a while and he claimed that she had laughed at him, telling him he looked funny with his stitched eyebrow and black eye. According to him, she kept saying that the other guy must have got the better of him in the fight and then she giggled.

Our Julie did have a bit of a nervous laugh so that
sounded quite plausible, although I'm sure she would-
n't have meant it maliciously. I doubt if she would have
risked making him angry if she knew even half of his
reputation for violence, which we could be pretty sure
she did. He claimed that he lost his temper at being
mocked, jumped up and strangled her right there in the
sitting room.

'I just lost it,' he kept saying.

So much for his dad's belief that he would never do
such a thing. The only part of the crime that he never
confessed to was about whatever he had done to her
vagina after she died; nor would he give any explanation as to how his semen might have got onto the blanket that she was wrapped in. Perhaps he thought that if
he made it sound like a murder committed in a moment
of blind temper it would go better for him than if there
was a sexual motive. Most people know what it feels like
to lose their temper, even if they would never go anywhere like as far as Billy, but defiling a dead body
would be beyond the understanding of all decent-minded
people.

Most of the people involved with prosecuting the case
didn't believe that part of his story. They thought it was
more likely he had attacked her in a sexual frenzy, having got himself worked up at the strip show. It seemed
likely he had gone round to Julie's hoping she would

sleep with him and when she refused he attacked her and killed her and then defiled her.

He said that when he realized she was dead he went out into the garden to look for somewhere to hide the body, but then lost his nerve and returned to the house. He claimed that he knew a bit about forensics because he'd been in trouble on a number of occasions before, and that made him decide to go upstairs and get a blanket off the bed. He then took off all his clothes, and all Julie's, wrapped her naked body in the blanket so he wouldn't be touching her and leaving any DNA, and carried her upstairs on his shoulder.

He said he thought about putting her up in the loft. He claimed he even climbed up on a set of drawers and tried to lift her through the hatch, but getting her that high was too awkward and she fell back on top of him. By that stage, if his version is true, he was getting desperate and it was then he hit on the idea of unscrewing the bath panel and hiding her behind the bath, planning to come back to get her another time. He gave a graphic description of how hard it was to force her body into such a confined space, pushing at her with his feet.

It was presumably because he planned to return for her that he took the keys with him, so that he could get back into the house whenever he wanted to. That also explained how it was that he had perhaps gone back into the house without forcing an entry, after the forensics team had gone, leaving the kitchen window open to make it look like a burglary.

He never explained what he'd done with the clothes Julie had been wearing that night, or with the wedding ring she still wore, but the bin men came the next day so perhaps he just put them in the bin. By the time the police started searching, the bins had been emptied and the evidence was destroyed long before they got there.

As his confession was related to us, I thought about that stocky man with the sullen, glowering face and I felt sick to the stomach that he had ever laid a finger on my beautiful daughter. He took off her clothes and touched her lovely skin; he pulled her wedding ring from her finger; and then he wrapped her in a blanket and carted her round her own house like an old piece of furniture that he was trying to store.

'We're going to get him for you, Julie,' I whispered in my head. 'If it's the last thing I ever do, I'll get him.'

Chapter Eighteen

Rolling out the Publicity

No matter how long I spent working with the police and others in authority, I still continued to be surprised by how little they seemed to take into account the feelings and needs of the relatives of murder victims. But I wasn't the only one who felt that way; many others were trying to improve the way things were done.

During this period the police introduced a pilot scheme in various parts of the country for something they called 'victims' impact statements'. What they wanted was for people like us to write statements that could be given to the judges before they passed sentence on the perpetrators of the crimes against us, to let them know the effect the crimes had had on our families. It seemed like a good idea, a way of humanizing the legal process a little and ensuring that judges received as rounded a view as possible.

The police asked us to write one of these statements for Billy's perjury trial, which I was keen to do if it would help to get him the maximum sentence possible. To be honest it was just nice to be asked, making it seem as if someone actually cared about what had happened to us and didn't just view us as an interesting legal case history.

Sitting down to write yet again about those traumatic days brought terrible flashbacks, transporting me back to the scene in the bathroom, but I was determined not to let them defeat me. I kept going, focusing all my energy into my pen, pouring everything I felt about Julie's murder and its effect on my family out onto paper.

Once the statement was finished Charlie and I took it to the head of the Crown Prosecution Service in our area to make sure it got directly into the judge's hands before he passed sentence. Writing it had been an ordeal but I felt sure it was going to prove to be worthwhile.

'I will personally make sure this gets to the judge in time,' he assured us.

Dunlop confessing had knocked me back in a way I would never have anticipated. It was as if I had been banging my head against a closed door and suddenly it had sprung open and I had fallen through without having any idea where I would land. I tried to keep going as normal but turning up at work at the hospital each day was finally becoming too much of a strain. It had been

good to keep going in the early years, to give myself
something else to think about other than Julie and Dunlop and to be with people who had other things to talk
about, but I eventually retired on medical grounds in
2000, after thirty years of doing the job.

In April 2000 Billy Dunlop appeared at the New
Court in Middlesborough and brazenly confessed to
Julie's murder, confirming everything he had said on the
prison tapes and in his confession to the police. It was a
staggering thing to do. He must have felt so totally safe
hiding behind the double jeopardy law that he believed
nothing else could touch him once he had served whatever time they gave him for perjury. It confirmed every
feeling I had that the law was ridiculous if it allowed a
man like this to get away with such a terrible crime.

He was sitting behind glass at the back of the courtroom, like a prize exhibit in the Chamber of Horrors.

'This man has made British legal history,' his defence
barrister trumpeted, as if it was something to be proud
of. 'No one has ever confessed in a court of law before,
after being acquitted for a killing. This man has confessed because he is full of remorse, especially for Julie's
family and her son.'

When the prosecuting counsel replied, he quite
rightly dismissed that claim as a load of rubbish. He said
he thought that all that had happened was that Dunlop
had taken legal advice and knew that there had been a

recommendation to look at the double jeopardy law after the MacPherson Report into the Stephen Lawrence case.

'He thinks that if he gets his confession in now he will only be charged with perjury and that will be the end of it for him. If or when the change of law comes in, he's assuming it won't be applied retrospectively.'

I didn't believe for a moment that Billy Dunlop felt any remorse towards us or anyone else. If he had felt remorse after the killing why did he go to so much trouble to hide Julie under the bath? If he had felt any pity for us at all during those three months when we were waiting for her to come home, he would have put in an anonymous phone call to the police, telling them where to find the body. He did none of that – just waited to see what he could get away with. Nothing I had heard during any of his court appearances had ever made me feel even the tiniest tremor of understanding or sympathy for what he had done. To me, Billy Dunlop was simply evil.

As I sat listening to the fatuous arguments being put forward in his defence it suddenly seemed like the most important thing in the world that he be given a full fourteen years for the perjury charges because then at least I would feel he was serving a decent sentence. Seeing him again in court, still behaving the same way, still alive while our Julie wasn't, re-ignited all my indignation and my determination to see him forced to pay a fair price for his crimes.

When the judge announced that he was only going to sentence Billy to six years for the perjury charge I felt all my hopes crumbling away. Although it meant he was going to be serving more prison time after he'd finished the sentence for attacking Donna and Shaun, it felt yet again as if he was getting away with something. How could it be that a man so evil and dangerous could continually be allowed to slip through the net, could continually be treated with leniency when he showed no leniency at all towards any of his victims?

As the judge's words rang in my ears a terrible uncontrollable rage swept over me at the realization that we were going to have to suffer yet another injustice on top of all the others. Unable to stop myself, I leapt to my feet and ran full tilt towards the dock with no idea what I would do when I got there. I just knew that I wanted to reach him, to hurt him as he had hurt us. Charlie tried to grab me but I was away like a rocket, leaving him with his arms flailing in the air. If I'd had a gun in my hand I would have shot Dunlop at that moment, protective glass or no protective glass.

'Six years?' I yelled at him. 'I'll see you rot in hell. You weren't full of remorse when you were sat in the house next door watching all the comings and goings. You murdering bastard!'

I was absolutely out of control, and I was lucky that the judge didn't hold me in contempt of court. The police and court officials finally managed to get a grip on me and calm me down. As I walked out of the building with Charlie, my mind was still whirling.

'If that's all he's going to get for perjury,' I said, 'then this change in the double jeopardy law needs to be looked at. I'm going to do something about this law.'

'You're wasting your time,' Charlie sighed, exhausted by the whole thing.

'I don't care.' I was adamant. 'I am going to do something about it.'

Fed up with being continually knocked back I was determined to take my cause to the very top. If I was going to get the law changed I was going to have to get to meet the people who actually had the power to do that. My first stop was to go back to our MP, Frank Cook, who had been so helpful in getting the police to talk to us.

'If I write a letter to Jack Straw, the Home Secretary, about our case,' I asked him the moment I had sat down in front of him, 'will you be able to get me in to see him?'

'I certainly will,' he said. 'You just bring me the letter.'

Encouraged by his positive attitude, I went straight home and wrote out the details of the case yet again, glad to have something to focus my mind on, to have a positive course to follow so I didn't have to sit around the house boiling in my own anger. I felt I could do something about this; one way or another I was going to get justice for our Julie.

From that moment on, the injustice of the double jeopardy law was constantly on my mind. Dealing with an 800-year-old law may sound dry and difficult to understand, but in fact the case we were putting forward was incredibly simple, particularly when looked at from our point of view. Anyone who had children could imagine how they would feel if they were in our position; they just needed to hear me tell our story in my own words. The problem was going to be getting in front of the right people in order to explain what had happened to us and to win them over to the cause.

The thing that had surprised me the most about the perjury trial was that the victims' impact statement I had written for the judge hadn't had more of an effect on the sentence he handed out. I wasn't willing to accept anything without question any more and wanted to find out what had been going on in his head, so I wrote to him expressing my surprise. I received a response by return of post saying that he had never seen the statement we had handed in to the head of the local Crown Prosecution Service. The Chief Crown Prosecutor had assured us he would pass it on and had failed to do so, possibly in some bureaucratic oversight. I couldn't believe we had been let down yet again. What was the point of asking victims for these statements if they weren't going to use them? Over and over again I felt that we were being told we didn't matter, that our suffering wasn't important enough for anyone to put themselves out.

With my new campaign under way I was always on the look out for allies, and if they were establishment figures so much the better. Lord Brian MacKenzie, the former president of the Police Superintendents' Association and a former Chief Superintendent of police in Durham, came on the television saying that when there's been a miscarriage of justice, whether it's a wrongful conviction or a wrongful acquittal, it should be looked at again. So I got in touch with him too. This was my new habit; whenever I heard anyone speaking out either for or against the idea of changing the law of double jeopardy, I immediately fired off a letter to them. It didn't matter how important or famous or grand they were; I knew they were mostly fathers and mothers just like us and I was banking on them being able to understand a heart-felt plea from another parent.

Although it was painful to have to talk about Julie's death in some ways, and any little reminder was still liable to bring on the flashbacks, I was keen to do any tele-vision or radio interviews or documentaries that came my way. I went on 'Tricia' and 'Woman's Hour' and all sorts of other programmes. I believed any media exposure that put across the emotional side of the argument to people who might not otherwise have thought about it was useful to the cause. Most ordinary people knew nothing about the double jeopardy law, unless they were involved in a case like ours or that of Stephen Lawrence's family. Anyone I explained it to was just as shocked and scandalized as I had been when I first learned about it. I was willing to do anything I had to in order to spread the word to as wide an audience as possible, which meant co-operating with the media whenever they offered any sort of potential platform.

By now I was so used to telling our story I could usually do it without becoming too upset, almost talking as though I was on automatic pilot, like an actress reciting a script she has learned by heart. I was often able to just set my mouth going and to cut off the painful thoughts lying behind my words. In a way I felt that I was keeping the memory of Julie alive at the same time. All the time I was talking about her, people were remembering her. People who would never have met her or heard about her had she lived, got to know her name and to hear of the great injustice that had been done to her.

I didn't expect anyone to call it 'Julie's Law' or anything like that, but if I could get it changed it would still be a legacy for her.

I think it's always better to be busy and distracted when you are trying to deal with a painful memory and this campaign gave me exactly the excuse I needed to be constantly rushing around lobbying people or talking to journalists. Charlie was always there at my side, quiet, determined and expressionless as ever, always supportive of whatever I did, if sometimes puzzled as to how I thought that two ordinary people like us would ever be able to make a difference to a law that had been on the statute books for nearly a millennium.

The producers of one documentary wanted to do a reconstruction of the morning when I went round to try to wake Julie up, and another of me pulling the panel off in the bathroom on that fateful day three months later. They talked about getting an actress to do the whole thing but I thought it would be just as hard for me to explain everything to another person as to get on and do it myself. I was quite frightened about the flashbacks it would cause, but I remembered how much better I had been after forcing myself into the bathroom on Martin's advice, so maybe this exercise would help to exorcise the flashbacks still further from the centre of my thoughts. I couldn't let these demons frighten me for the rest of my life; I had to stand up and face them.

'It's OK,' I told the television people. 'I can do it myself.'

We didn't use the actual house because the woman who lived there by then had a little boy and we didn't think that would be nice for him, so we borrowed the one next door from Mark Ward's mum, Kath. I have to admit that as I was re-enacting it, banging on the door and shouting Julie's name through the letterbox, it did bring back some of the pain, but I had to shut my mind off and keep going. The first time I tried the handle to the front door, Kath had forgotten to lock it so it came open to my touch and I fell in, which took away some of the tension, making us all laugh.

The bathroom scene was filmed in the producer's house where there was a room big enough to fit a whole camera crew as well as me. They'd hired an actress to play Julie under the bath but she'd put some weight on since the producer had last seen her and there was no way they were going to be able to cram her in there. They had to use the producer's thirteen-year-old son instead and get him to put a wig on. It seemed almost unreal that I could be laughing about something that had so devastated my life, but I think perhaps that is all part of the healing process – learning how to live with what has happened and beginning to see it in perspective. I know Julie herself would have been giggling away if she'd been watching the whole farce. The final result was very effective when we saw it on screen.

The actor they'd hired to play Billy looked exactly like him and it was chilling to watch him carrying the body up the stairs, making real a scene that had played

out in my imagination a million times. He must have
been able to see the expression of shock on my face when
I first walked into the kitchen and saw him.

'I'm not him, you know,' he said quickly.

Maybe he was worried I was going to fly at him. He
must have been a good actor because when they went on
to film the scene in the rugby club, where Dunlop got
drunk and gave the stripper a hard time, he was so convincing that a member of the public took exception and
butted into the scene.

'I don't like your attitude, mate!' he said, punching
the poor actor in the face before the television crew were
able to explain what was happening.

A German television company wanted to do a debate
on double jeopardy as well, and wanted to come over to
make a short film to open the programme. Mark Braithwaite, with whom I was still in regular contact, advised
me to do it because if our campaign to change the law
failed in the UK and we had to go to the European
Court of Human Rights there might be German judges
on the panel and it might be helpful to influence public
opinion over there if we had a chance to do so.

A lot of people in the legal profession opposed the
idea of changing the double jeopardy law and I had to
try to lobby every one of them and explain why I
thought they were wrong. One of them, surprisingly,
was Imran Khan, the lawyer who had worked on the

Stephen Lawrence case and who I thought should have been on our side. I talked to him on camera for a television programme. His main argument was that changing the law would lead to sloppy police work because the police would know that if they made mistakes they could keep on bringing suspects back for re-trial as often as they wanted. But I had already read the proposals that were being put forward and I knew there were going to be safeguards built in to stop that kind of thing.

I also knew he had a daughter, because he'd mentioned it earlier, so I went for the personal angle.

'Do you have any family?' I asked as the cameras rolled.

'Yes, I do,' he admitted.

'If your daughter had been murdered,' I said, 'and a man had confessed in a court of law to the killing, would you be happy with a perjury sentence? I don't mean as a lawyer, I mean as a father.'

He started to waffle again.

'Just answer the question – yes or no,' I insisted. I'd spent so much time sitting listening to lawyers in courtrooms that I was even starting to talk like them. 'As a father, would you be happy?'

'No,' he said, 'of course I wouldn't.'

'Then you can stop the cameras,' I said, 'because that answers it all. As a lawyer he's opposing changes but as a father he wouldn't be happy with a perjury sentence. We are willing to go to the European Court of Human Rights if necessary to get justice for our daughter.'

I was getting quite good at this campaigning and debating business, surprising even myself sometimes. It's amazing what you can do when you have to.

A while before Billy was sent down for perjury I lost my purse in town and I rang the police station to report it. It seemed strange to be reporting something so relatively trivial after all I had been through with them over the years. They sent out a policeman and woman to take a statement and the man had the brim of his cap pulled right down over his nose when he arrived, as if he was trying to hide. The woman was doing all the talking and I kept peering at the man as I listened, certain that I recognized him from somewhere.

'I'm sure I know you, don't I?' I said eventually.

Without a word he slid the cap up and I immediately knew who it was.

'PC Newman,' I said, remembering the young officer who had first told me that Julie was exactly the type of girl to go running off to London, leaving her kid behind. 'Community relations extraordinaire.'

'Not any more, I'm not,' he said, his face turning beetroot. 'I'm just an ordinary copper on the beat now. A few heads have rolled because of your case. I'll always regret the words I said to you that day.'

'It was your attitude that I objected to,' I said, still not quite able to let it go, even though I couldn't help feeling a bit sorry for the poor lad. 'You were so sure you knew better than me, even though I was the mother talking about her daughter and you were a policeman dealing with a stranger.'

Around 2001, I joined a support group called Support After Murder and Manslaughter (SAMM) and at one of their meetings, I got talking to a police officer who asked if I would be interested in addressing police officers as part of their family liaison training. By explaining to them what it is like on our side of the fence, hopefully officers will gain more insight. On one occasion I went to visit a bereaved family with a senior investigating officer and we got talking on the way.

'You won't remember me,' the officer said on the way there, 'but the day you found your Julie I was a young constable and I'd just been transferred to Billingham. It was my first shift and the first call I got was to come to 27 Grange Avenue. All I remember was you out in the street, hysterical.'

'The day when I punched Inspector Lee, you mean?' I chuckled.

'It really upset me,' he went on, ignoring my flippant interruption, 'because I had a family and I could imagine exactly how you must be feeling. I went home that night and I said to my wife, "It was terrible; this poor woman was hysterical from finding her daughter." It was awful.' His words caught in his throat at the recollection.

I could see that Julie's death and everything that happened after it had changed a lot of people's lives, not just ours. But I wanted it to change a lot more than that. I wanted it to change the way justice was dispensed in Britain in the future, and for that to happen I was going to have to keep up the pressure on everyone I met. Now that I was learning more about how the law worked I was no longer doing it just to see Billy Dunlop fairly sentenced for what he had done. I wanted to achieve something bigger than that, something that would potentially help everyone.

Chapter Nineteen

Telling Kevin

Journalists and headline writers like to label murders with catchy phrases that will remind readers forever more about that specific tragic event. Whenever Dunlop was back in the news the local press would print headlines like 'Body behind the bath murder' or they would talk about the 'Pizza delivery girl killing'. I didn't like to see Julie's whole life reduced to such clichés, but I soon realized there was nothing I could do about it. When you are the victim of a gruesome murder you somehow seem to become public property. Whenever another of these stories appeared, kids at Kevin's school would start talking about it, passing around snippets of information that they must have got from their parents or maybe overheard in a shop or on the street somewhere. Ten years after his mother's murder, we had still not told Kevin anything other than the story that she had slipped and died in the bath.

He used to live with Andrew during the week but he spent virtually every weekend and holiday of his childhood with us. Andrew had met a new partner quite soon after parting from Julie and Kevin soon had two half brothers. Everyone got on well with one another, even though there was always this secret hanging in the air when we were together and Kevin was in the room. There was a whole section of our lives that we couldn't talk about when he was around, which was always a strain since it was a subject that was never far from the fronts of our minds. In some ways, perhaps it was healthy for us to have to talk about other things when he was around, to think about him and his future and not to dwell all the time on the tragedies of the past.

In 1999, when Kevin was thirteen, the case was back in the papers again because of the approaching perjury trial. I told Andrew I really thought he should talk to him about it, but he still wasn't keen. I suppose after ten years he didn't want to have to rake up so many painful memories for himself as well as giving Kevin things to think about that he might not be able to cope with.

'Unless he asks,' Andrew said, 'I'm not going to tell him.'

Kevin was very close to Charlie and they used to go away together sometimes for breaks. Afterwards

Charlie would tell me how Kevin would often ask him questions such as 'What does "murder" mean exactly?' And once he said, 'I've been dreaming about me mam and in me dream she was in a coffin on the drive and she had a big mark down her face.'

All the time he was talking, he would be looking at Charlie as if trying to read his grandfather's reactions to his words. But Charlie's face was never an easy one for anyone to read. Kevin started to write little notes about his mam dying and then he would leave them around the place as if by accident for us to find. But still he didn't seem to want to come out and ask the questions bluntly.

One afternoon the school welfare officer came round unexpectedly and asked if she could talk to us. Alarmed, we invited her in and she told us that Kevin had been to see her at school that day.

'He said that other children have been telling him that his mum didn't slip in the bath,' she said, 'that she'd been murdered. Now he says he's going to find out the truth for himself.'

'I'm going to go to the library,' he told her, 'and I'm going to look in the archives of the paper and see what I can find out.'

Aware how Andrew felt about Kevin being told, she hadn't said anything to him but she had come straight round to see us so that we would be forewarned. I realized then that we couldn't lie to the lad any more. I rang

243

Andrew and he came round to talk to the welfare officer himself.

'I don't want to tell him unless he asks,' he still insisted.

'But he isn't going to ask,' she explained. 'He told me he didn't want to ask any of you in case he upsets anybody. But he wants to know the truth.'

I could see that Andrew was wavering. She was forcing him to think it through, which he had probably been avoiding ever since it happened, and he was realizing she was right. Eventually he went home to find Kevin and asked him straight out what it was he wanted to know.

'Was me mam murdered?' Kevin asked.

'Yes, she was,' Andrew replied. 'By a man called Billy Dunlop.'

'Why did he murder her?'

'Who knows why somebody murders another person?' Andrew said. 'I don't know why.'

'I want to go back to my Nana's,' Kevin said.

Over the years I had been building up a scrapbook of newspaper cuttings, which I had always thought I would give to him one day so he could read for himself what had happened. When he came round I gave it to him and he sat reading for a while. I could see his heart was broken and I just wanted to hug him and make the pain all go away. I knew exactly what he felt like because I had been experiencing the same thoughts and feelings myself for ten years by then.

'Nana,' he said, 'I never wanted to ask in case talking about it upset you, but now I know the truth I feel like a weight has been lifted from me shoulders. Is the man who did it in prison?'

'Yes, he is,' I said.

'Is he in prison for what he did to me mam?'

'No,' I said, 'he isn't, but we hope to change that.'

For a while he went quiet and I didn't know where to start with telling him everything that had gone on behind the newspaper stories. I still wasn't sure how much he needed to know and how much he would prefer not to think or talk about yet. I decided I needed some professional help in case we did him some psychological damage, so I got in touch with a London-based organization called Mothers Against Murder and they told me about a specialized counselling service in Sunderland, which was only about half an hour up the road. Kevin agreed that I could take him there. He got on well with them and went back every week for over a year, seeming to find it helpful. He said that now he knew what had happened it was much easier to talk openly to his friends at school.

Looking back now, I believe it is always better to tell children the basic truth from the start in traumatic situations like murder, however hard that might be at the time, then they feel able to ask more questions once they are ready to understand more.

We only found out recently that after hearing the truth, Kevin went back on his own to the house where it happened and knocked on the door, asking the new people there if he could come in and try to remember his mam. They very kindly let him in and he looked round the house, even though it must have changed a lot. He told us later that he still couldn't remember Julie at all. I know he finds that hard. Every lad would like to be able to remember his mother, to know where he came from.

Most of his memories are just things that Charlie and I have talked to him about over the years, stories we've told him about when he was a baby, or when Julie was a child. Everyone needs to have some family history, something they can feel they belong to and are a part of. I expect it got even harder for Andrew to talk to Kevin about Julie when he had a new partner and family, but it was the right thing to do in the end.

Once he knew the truth, Kevin became an active part of our campaign team, often travelling with us to see people who we thought might be able to help the cause and willing to speak out to anyone who would listen. It helped the emotional argument for people to be able to hear directly from a boy who had been left motherless when he was only three years old. He became as eager to see his mother's killer brought to justice as Charlie and I were. Month by month and year by year I felt we were building up more and more support by constantly writing to people and talking about the cause, but I knew we were still a long way from our goal. I knew that as a family we had to keep up the pressure right until the day we heard a judge pronounce Billy Dunlop guilty of murder and sentence him to life, however exhausted and dispirited we might sometimes feel along the way.

Chapter Twenty

Making Friends
in High Places

Just as he promised, Frank Cook arranged a meeting for us with Jack Straw at the Home Office and we set off to London. I took with me a picture of Julie and a picture of Dunlop. What's that saying – 'A picture's worth a thousand words'? I think that is definitely true. Just looking at her pretty young face and his glowering, evil stare would bring the whole story instantly to life for anyone.

I didn't have mountains of notes; this was going to be an appeal to the Home Secretary's emotions as a father, not his intellect as a politician or a barrister. As we headed up to the top floor in the lift, Frank suggested that I let him do all the talking. He probably thought he was reassuring me, expecting me to be nervous and tongue-tied in front of such a famous and powerful man. I didn't say anything but I've never been known to sit quiet and I had no intention of doing so this time either.

Jack Straw, such a familiar face from news bulletins ever since Tony Blair's government came to power in 1997, greeted us and led us into his office. God alone knows how many hands a man like that shakes in the course of an average day. Before Frank could open his mouth I placed the two pictures on the desk in front of the Home Secretary. His eyes went straight to them and I knew I had his full attention.

'That's our daughter, Julie,' I said, 'and that's the man who murdered her. He's confessed to it in a court of law and I want to know what's going to be done about this double jeopardy law. He's making a complete mockery of the British justice system.'

'Well,' he said, reaching for a big thick law book, 'you know, retrospective law is a very grey area.'

'Don't bother to touch that book,' I warned, 'because there is no case in that book like ours. Am I right?'

'Well, yes, you are …'

'His defence lawyer admitted in court that Dunlop's made British legal history,' I ploughed on. 'So this law needs to be looked at.'

Frank had given up and sat back by this time, realizing there was nothing he could do to stop me having my say. Any control he had hoped to keep over the proceedings was long gone. I hoped he wasn't regretting helping me to get this far.

'The Home Affairs Select Committee have already held a debate,' Straw purred, 'and they are recommending it be changed and they've also suggested it would apply to retrospective cases but there's a long way to go.'

I could see he was doubtful about being able to change the double jeopardy law to apply to retrospective cases such as ours, so I felt things would move very slowly.

'What's the next step?' I wanted to know.

'It goes to the Law Commission.'

'Right,' I said, gathering up my photographs. 'I'll have the name of whoever's dealing with it in the Law Commission.'

'My secretary will sort that out for you,' he assured me, probably quite keen to get me out of his office by that stage.

That was pretty much the end of the interview, but it had got me what I wanted. I now knew that there were some very important people thinking about changing the double jeopardy law. All I had to do now was make sure they hurried up and came to the right conclusion. It would be a disaster if they all sat around talking about it for years and then decided that the law had been good enough for eight centuries so there was no need to change it now. It would be equally disastrous for my family if they changed the law but did not make it retrospective. Julie would still have her legacy if that happened, but we would never be able to get the justice she deserved for Billy Dunlop. As we left Straw's office his secretary told us the name I needed was a judge on the panel called Alan Wilkie. She gave me his address.

'I'm going to write to this Law Commission,' I told Charlie once we were back home on the sofa, having a cup of tea and thinking what to do next.

'You're wasting your time,' Charlie half-heartedly protested yet again. The poor man just wanted a bit of a rest.

'I'm doing it,' I said. 'I don't care what anybody says.'

I sat back down at the dining table that evening and outlined the whole case yet again, copied everything the next day, and then sent it all off to Judge Alan Wilkie.

A few days later I received a lovely letter back from him, bringing with it the first definite glimmer of hope. He told me my letter had arrived at a crucial time, just as the Law Commission were getting their thoughts together to recommend changes to the double jeopardy law and its application to retrospective cases. He said ours was the most compelling case in the country. He asked if we would like to meet him. That was an invitation I wasn't likely to pass up on. If there was one thing I had learned on my journey so far it was never to turn down an opportunity to look these important people directly in the eye. You can write letters till you are blue in the face and still not be sure that you have got your point across effectively, but if we were actually sitting in front of them, making them think about how it felt to be in our position, we could make sure we didn't leave until they understood exactly what should happen. As long as they were hiding behind secretaries and oak-panelled offices they could act as grand and magnanimous as they liked, but when they were confronted with a bereaved mother armed with photographs they were reminded that such things could happen to any parent, including them.

In the meantime, back down in the real world of police, courts, solicitors and prisons, Dunlop had been given the right to appeal against his six-year sentence. By this time 'victims' impact statements' had become the law and the police asked us to write another one. Although I was still seething that the last one I'd written had never even been sent to the judge by the Crown Prosecution Service, I was willing to have another try, so I wrote the whole thing out again, just as before, and the police came to the house to collect it.

Having been let down so often before, however, I didn't trust them to pass it on to the right people, so I got the case file number from one of the perjury team and a while later I phoned the clerk of the court. He gave me the name of the man looking after the Dunlop file. When I got through I asked him if he would mind looking to see if my impact statement was in there. He promised to call me back as soon as he had looked.

'There is no impact statement in this file,' he told me when he phoned back later.

I immediately rang the head of the Crown Prosecution Service, my blood boiling, spoiling for a fight.

'He's in a meeting,' they told me when I got through.

'Then you can go into that meeting and tell him I am going to be down there in half an hour to pick up my impact statement,' I told them. 'You let me down when Dunlop was first charged with perjury and now you've done the same again for the Court of Appeal.'

Ten minutes later I got another phone call from the clerk at the Court of Appeal.

'I don't know who you've spoken to or what you've done,' my contact said, 'but we've just had your impact statement faxed to us.'

The fact that they failed to pass ours on twice suggests that the authorities really don't understand just how important these impact statements (they're now called 'victims' personal statements'), are to the families of murder victims. Even if our words don't make any difference to the sentence that a judge eventually hands out to a murderer, it still makes us feel better to know that they have at least read and considered what we have to say. My experience from the day Julie first disappeared suggests that most people in official jobs are unable to put themselves into the shoes of the victims' families unless they are forced to.

Maybe police and legal officials believe they wouldn't be able to cope with their jobs if they weren't able to distance themselves from the emotional arguments in cases like ours, but I think it is more likely that they would do their jobs far more effectively if they listened a bit more closely to what we all have to say. If the people at the Crown Prosecution Service had realized how important it was for us to have the judges read those statements, they would never have been so careless about sending them across.

The appeal meant Dunlop was going to be brought back into the courtroom and, since Charlie and I refused to miss a single move he made in public, we were going to have to sit through the whole thing again. This time it was going to happen down in London, so Alan Wilkie suggested that if we were going to come down anyway we should have a meeting with him at the Law Commission offices in Holborn the day before. This was another opportunity too good to turn down.

When we arrived I assumed we were just going to be taken in to meet him, but as we entered the room we found ourselves being seated before the full panel, including a man called Jacques Perry, who was the head of the enquiry. We all sat round a big table, drinking tea, and they were absolutely charming.

'Off the record,' Alan Wilkie told us, 'there wasn't a dry eye on this panel when we got your letter, because we're all fathers. We all know how we would feel if it was our son or daughter who had been murdered.'

'I just want to bring the human side of things into the debate,' I said.

'Can we use your letter to take to the government?' he asked.

'Never mind me letter,' I said, 'you can use me. This law needs to be changed. We've met a number of other families in a similar position to us and there are about thirty-five cases around the country where people are desperate for this law to change so that justice can be done. When there's been a proven wrongful conviction the person is immediately set free, so surely the same should apply with a proven wrongful acquittal?'

At the end of the meeting they told us to leave everything with them and I refocused my mind on preparing myself to go to the Court of Appeal the next day. I hated the thought of having to see Dunlop again, even when he was in handcuffs and behind glass or bars, but there was no way I wasn't going to be there to hear what went on. I was terrified something would go wrong and the previous decision would be reversed, allowing him back out again. I knew we weren't alone; there were a lot of people in Billingham who were frightened of the idea of Billy Dunlop being allowed back out onto the streets amongst them.

When we got to the court in the morning we found that Jacques Perry, the head of the Law Commission who we'd met the day before, was also in there, watching just like us. He came straight over and gave me a cuddle as though we were the oldest friends in the world.

'I didn't expect you to come today,' I confessed.

'Oh yes,' he said. 'We're very interested in Mr Dunlop's case.'

The three judges presiding over the court were not impressed by the appeal and to our relief it was dismissed in just a few minutes. They also mentioned our impact statement and it made me feel better to know that they had actually read it. Billy was expressionless as always but we hoped he was listening and that he knew just how hard we were working to keep him behind bars.

'So what happens next?' I asked Jacques Perry once we were back outside the court.

'We'll do our consultation paper,' he explained. 'And we'll send you a copy on the day it's published. After that it's got to go to the Lord Justice Auld for his consideration.'

I got back on the train home that evening feeling that maybe we were finally making some progress. Something was actually going in our favour. The wheels were certainly moving slowly, but Dunlop was safely behind bars, which gave us the time we needed to go through all these different layers of the legal system. I was determined to keep pushing until I got there, however long it took and however many people I had to go and see.

True to their word the Law Commission sent us a copy of the paper on the day it was published in January 2001, and then the judiciary and legislators thought about it – for two and a half years.

We were back to living in a state of limbo, with no idea which way things were likely to go, but by now we were used to it. We were getting so close to seeing our dream come true that nothing would have stopped us. The main thing in our favour was that at least Dunlop was locked up for a good few years because he couldn't start serving his perjury sentence until he had completed his sentence for grievous bodily harm to Shaun and Donna. The earliest he could possibly be released was April 2006, but there were times while the legal establishment was pondering when I wondered if they would manage to reach a decision in time to save us from Dunlop's release from prison.

All through those years I never rested and never became complacent. We had been disappointed and let down too many times before to believe that anything concerning the law was certain. The fight for justice occupied my thoughts from the moment I woke in the early mornings to the moment I finally went to sleep, and it still kept me awake most nights.

There were dozens of different debates going on down in Whitehall and Frank Cook was brilliant at keeping us informed at every stage, telling us who was chairing what meeting and whether or not it had come out in our favour. I would then get in touch with whoever it was, thanking them if they had been positive, and trying to explain to them why they were wrong if they had been negative. I wrote to the head of the Bar Council, sending a video of one of the television programmes we'd made, but he sent it straight back without comment. I knew I could never win them all, but I just wanted to do everything I could to keep the ball rolling and gather support wherever I could find it.

So many years were passing that contacts we had made at the beginning of the campaign moved on and were replaced by new people, meaning we had to start all over again. Jack Straw left the Home Office in one of Tony Blair's reshuffles in 2001 to become Foreign Secretary and was replaced by David Blunkett, the former Education Secretary, so I prepared another letter for the new Home Secretary to make sure that he knew all about the case. I was worried that he would have agendas of his own and wouldn't be interested in anything that had been done by his predecessor.

I found a blind lady in Middlesborough who translated my letter into braille, so that he had no excuse not to read it himself. I didn't have any confidence that anyone else would read it to him. It was worth going to that extra little bit of trouble because he wrote back to say that he was committed to carrying on with the Law Commission's recommendations. We breathed a huge sigh of relief; we were still in business.

Finally, after two and a half years, Lord Justice Auld announced that not only was the law to be changed but that it might apply retrospectively in particular cases. We were one step closer to actually seeing the law change. It seemed as though we were inching our way forward despite all the setbacks and delays and all the years that had passed since we started on our journey. Sometimes it felt a bit like being back at school as I learned more about the way our legal and political systems worked every day.

The bill went through the Houses of Parliament and was put into a white paper released in July 2002, entitled 'Justice for All'. (A white paper is a document that lays out a new policy and signifies the government's intention to introduce it as legislation.) David Blunkett actually wrote to us and arranged for us to collect our copy of the white paper on the day it was published. We arrived at the Home Office at 3.30 in the afternoon and found that the press officer had very kindly stuck a post-it note on the front that read 'Double jeopardy will be retrospective'. I burst into tears as I read it. The press were all waiting outside and I ran out shouting the news at the top of my voice.

The bill was then dragged through many more debates; some people were in favour of the changes and others were still vehemently opposing them. I was constantly searching for new people in influential positions who I could win round to our point of view, people to whom I could explain the human side of the story. Often the debates were all about dry, ancient points of law and had nothing to do with the reality of Julie lying dead under the bath and Dunlop being able to boast to all and sundry in the pub that he had committed the perfect murder.

Having got the Criminal Justice Bill through the House of Commons in May 2003, we then had to get it past the House of Lords, which I was told was going to be the really tough one. The first debate in the Lords went okay but we still weren't home and dry.

All this time Charlie and I had been busy on every possible front. We'd made another documentary, met what felt like a thousand new people, and every year we went to a conference in South Shields for the North East of England Victims' Association. That year one of the guest speakers was Tony Blair's friend Lord Falconer, who was Constitutional Affairs Secretary and Lord Chancellor and seemed to have taken on the job of 'Victims' Minister' at the time.

At one stage during the lunch break he got up and walked past our table towards the door. I had been coiled like a spring for some time, waiting for an opportunity like this. I watched his approach from the corner of my eye, ready to pounce the moment he got close enough. As soon as he was within reach I jumped up and grabbed his arm, dragging the startled man down into a seat beside me and explaining who I was as quickly as I could before he had a chance to get up and run for his life.

'Lord Falconer, can you help me?' I begged. 'We're desperate for the double jeopardy law to be changed. I know it's got to go through a second debate, so can I come to the House of Lords and speak to the people who are going to be debating it?'

'Would you do that?' he asked, obviously surprised that anyone would want to volunteer themselves for such an ordeal.

'I will if you can organize it.'

'All right,' he nodded, smiling. 'I'll be in touch.'

Within a week I got a call from Frank Cook saying I had an appointment to go to the House of Lords. It often surprised me how good people right at the top of the Establishment tree were at doing what they promised, while those lower down the ladder were constantly letting us down. I suppose that's one of the reasons why some people reach the top while others never will, but I guess they also have lots of staff to do their bidding once they get there, which makes it easier to carry out their promises.

We were so nearly within reach of our goal now; we couldn't afford to let this opportunity slip through our fingers. After all these years of waiting the thought of failing at the last fence was unbearable. I wanted to ensure I was completely prepared.

I sat down at the dining room table once again and wrote out a five-page outline that would be my statement to this final bunch of grandees, giving all the reasons why I thought the law should change and why it should be made retrospective. I was going to be appealing unashamedly to their hearts as well as their heads. By the time I'd finished I was pleased with what I'd done – Lord knows I'd had enough practice by then – and I got some copies printed off the next day. The following is what I finally wrote, telling our story for what I hoped would be the last time.

> To whom it may concern.
> This is the catalogue of errors that occurred in our case which eventually led me to campaign to change the double jeopardy law:
>
> November 16th 1989 I reported to Cleveland Police our eldest daughter Julie (age 22) was missing from home. I was adamant that Julie had disappeared mysteriously and a gut feeling told me something dreadful had happened to her. The police suggested

she might have 'taken off to London to start a new life' knowing her young son Kevin, age 3, was being looked after by me. Due to my insistence a team of so-called 'forensic officers' went to search Julie's house five days after I reported her missing. The team spent five days in the house; at the end of this search we were told by the D.I. he could guarantee that nothing untoward had happened to Julie in that house. As all Julie's keys were missing the police changed the lock on the back door. They kept the new key for some eighty days. In all this time there was no contact from Julie.

Jan 31st 1990 the police decided to give the key to my son-in-law Andrew. He intended to move back into the house with Kevin.

1st Feb 1990 Andrew switched on the central heating system and, noticing a 'horrible' smell coming from the bathroom, he phoned me. I suggested he put some bleach down the toilet as it had not been used for nearly three months. Andrew was only in the house for a couple of hours to clean off the fingerprint dust.

5th Feb 1990 I called at the house at lunchtime with Kevin to see if Andrew had got rid of the smell. As he opened the door he said it was getting worse. As I walked into the house I smelled the putrid smell. Having worked in an operating theatre for over twenty years,

I knew what the smell was but inside I was praying 'Please God, don't let it be Julie.' I entered the bathroom. As I leaned across the bath to smell the wall my knees pressed against the bath panel and the pungent smell became stronger. The bath panel had always been loose at one end so I bent down and pulled it open. There, to my horror, was my daughter's decomposing body, which the police team had failed to find.

Feb 14th 1990 Billy Dunlop was arrested and charged with Julie's murder. He denied this.

Forensic evidence against him.
- Julie's keys found nailed under the floorboards in the house where Dunlop was lodging.
- Three fingerprints, all Dunlop's, found on the key fob.
- Fibres from the jumper Dunlop wore the night Julie was killed found on the blanket that he had partly covered Julie's body with.
- Hairs from Dunlop's head found on the blanket.
- Semen with a partial DNA match to Dunlop was found on the blanket.

With all this forensic evidence, a jury at the first trial failed to reach a decision so Judge Swinton-Thomas ordered a re-trial.

At the re-trial Judge Harry Ognall gave the jury just five hours to deliberate, so a second jury failed to reach a decision and Dunlop was acquitted.

Within weeks of his acquittal Dunlop was boasting in public houses he had 'got away with the perfect murder'. People were phoning us so we went to the police, who also had been told. At this point the police said nothing could be done about Dunlop because of 'double jeopardy'.

Several years later Dunlop was charged with threats to kill the woman he was living with and received a custodial sentence.

A few months after that Dunlop was charged with attempted murder of a man and woman. He pleaded not guilty but guilty to grievous bodily harm. He was only given a seven-year sentence, even though he hit the man so hard that he snapped a baseball bat on his face. He stabbed the woman thirteen times with an oven fork.

Whilst in prison for the above offences he sent a death threat letter to the woman in which he said that upon his release he would do to her what he did to Julie. He admitted in the letter that he did kill Julie. He also confessed to a prison officer. The police put a tape on the officer and Dunlop described in great detail how he killed Julie and concealed her body.

Once again, because of 'double jeopardy' he couldn't be charged with killing Julie. He was only charged with perjury, that he lied twice in court, so for two counts of perjury (maximum sentence for each count was seven years) Dunlop was only given six years in total.

His defence barrister said that Dunlop had made 'British legal history', being the first person to have been acquitted of murder then later to confess 'in court'. If this is the case there are no guidelines, no test case, so please set a precedent with this case. Change the 'double jeopardy' law. Make it retrospective and instead of criminals like Dunlop making a complete mockery of the British justice system let Dunlop and others be brought to justice for the crime he has confessed to, not just for lying in court for this horrendous crime.

I will challenge any civil liberties group about 'human rights'. Our daughter had a right to life. Dunlop took this from her. We have a right for justice for Julie and the only way for us and other families to obtain justice is to:

Change the 'double jeopardy' law.
Retrospectively.
Yours sincerely,
Ann and Charlie Ming and Family

We arrived in London on 9 July 2003 and yet again we took a taxi from the station to the Houses of Parliament, a building that looks daunting as you approach it but at the same time so familiar from a thousand news stories. Frank Cook met us in the lobby and introduced us to Lord Goldsmith, the Attorney General, who was going to be chairing the meeting and had a briefcase bulging with papers.

'Do you have any notes with you?' he asked, eyeing my slim statement suspiciously.

'No,' I said, tapping my head. 'It's all stored in my grey matter.'

'Will you be all right?' He seemed concerned.

'I'll be perfectly all right,' I assured him.

He led the way into a room where there was a table that was practically the size of our whole flat set up for our meeting, and he showed us to our seats. As the lords started filing in I felt a tremor of anxiety. There were walking sticks and zimmer frames and hearing aids all over the place and I couldn't help wondering how the debate was going to go. These people didn't look as though they were going to like the idea of retrospective law changes in the least. I spotted the familiar face of Lord Mackenzie amongst them. An elderly baroness plonked herself down on the chair next to me.

'I do hope you are going to speak up, my dear,' she said loudly.

'I'll do my best,' I promised. 'I'll talk to your good ear.'

'I don't have a good ear,' she said.

'Then I'll shout.'

Once everyone was in and seated, Lord Goldsmith introduced me to the rest of them and I focused myself on what was going on. I knew this was my last chance to put the message across effectively before the final decisions would be taken. If we didn't get it past the Lords we were going to end up having to go to the European Court in Brussels, which would make everything a hundred times more complicated and frustrating. It was hard enough travelling up and down to London, never mind going back and forth across the Channel to Belgium.

As I talked to these learned and distinguished people about our Julie and about Billy Dunlop I became so passionate that I did go off at a bit of a tangent, just using my statement as a prompt, but they seemed to stay with me despite all the hearing aids. I assumed it must have gone OK because at the end of the meeting the Chief Whip asked if I would mind if she gave a copy of my statement to everybody in the House of Lords.

Lord Goldsmith thanked me for coming and explained that they would now be looking at all the safeguards they were going to need to insert into the law once double jeopardy had been removed in order to make it really sound, so there would be a couple of small debates before the second big one. He promised to send me copies of all of them.

'You've forgotten one little word, Lord Goldsmith,' I said.

'One little word?'

'Yes, "retrospective".'

They all laughed because by then they had got the message as to just how desperate I was to get it done right. If the changes did not allow cases from the past to be re-tried then we would never be able to get Billy back into court. True to his word, Lord Goldsmith sent me copies of all the debates from then on and it felt strange to read about these senior law lords saying things like 'and I quote Ann Ming', with chunks of my statement then reproduced as if I was one of them. It was like reading about someone else.

Soon after that trip to London I bumped into one of the surgeons I used to work with when I was a theatre nurse, and he asked me how I was getting on with my campaign. I gave him as brief an outline as I could manage of all the things we had been doing, including the trip to the House of Lords.

'How did you find the courage to go down there and speak to those people?' he asked.

'After working with you,' I laughed, 'the lords were pussy cats.'

270

Immediately after the second debate had taken place, Frank Cook rang us.

'It's my birthday today,' he said, 'and it's been the best one I've ever had. The changes are through and they are going to apply to retrospective cases.'

I couldn't believe I was hearing him right. After waiting and fighting for so long, was it really just going to happen like that? Were we actually going to see a change in the law which would mean we could start to demand that Dunlop be retried for killing our Julie? It was hard to take in his words and, after so many years of trying to hold in the tears in order to get my message across, I wasn't able to stem them any longer. The relief washed over me like a tidal wave.

Not that we were going to be able to march straight back into the courtroom. First we had to wait for the new law to get through to the statute books, which was going to take another year – but that was nothing after having waited so long to get this far.

Lord Falconer was at another victims' conference a while later and I spotted him talking to the press outside the building. I went over to thank him for all he'd done to help.

'Well done you,' he boomed as soon as he saw me. 'What an achievement!'

'And well done you,' I replied as he enveloped me a great big cuddle, 'for getting me the appointment.'

271

I did feel proud of what we had achieved, but at the same time I did wonder why I'd had to fight so hard every inch of the way just to get basic justice for Julie, something that people in a free country should be able to take for granted. Julie was murdered and Dunlop had admitted to doing it; the legal system should have taken over from there without us having to go through so much.

When the Queen next opened parliament she was going to talk about changing the double jeopardy law and Tyne Tees Television took Charlie and me down to London to film us listening to her. It was hard to believe that our struggle had actually got all the way up to the Queen of England; we were part of something that was going to be going down in the history books.

'At the heart of my Government's legislative pro-gramme,' she was saying in her familiar voice, 'is a commitment to reform and rebalance the criminal justice system to deliver justice for all and to safeguard the interests of victims, witnesses and communities.' Her words were going past me as if in a dream. 'The Bill will also allow retrials for those acquitted of serious offences where new and compelling evidence emerges.'

I was surprised how moving I found it. After waiting for so many years to hear the words that she was now speaking so matter-of-factly, it was bringing tears to my eyes. Even at this stage I was still frightened that something might happen that would mean a change of government and everything being put back yet again, but we were closer than we had ever been to being in a position to get Billy Dunlop retried for the things he did that night in 1989. I could allow myself once more to dream about hearing him sentenced to life for murder, when I had begun to fear I would not live long enough to see it made possible.

Chapter Twenty-one

The Final Verdict

On 4 April 2006 the law actually changed and became enforceable retrospectively. On 5 April the local Chief Crown Prosecutor rang us and asked if we would like to go in for a meeting with him.

'There's still a long way to go,' he warned when we arrived. 'We have to get the paperwork out and go through everything again, but hopefully within a couple of months we will get it all polished off and down to the head of the Department of Public Prosecutions.'

He explained that he would have to get Dunlop's original acquittal quashed before another trial could begin, and that because it was a landmark ruling case there would be five high court judges in attendance, all of them the highest judges in the land.

'They probably won't make a final decision the same day,' he warned. 'Once they've heard the case they'll most likely ask you to come back again in two weeks or so, once they've had time to think about it.'

Although we were now definitely heading in the right direction I knew that things could still go wrong because it had happened so many times in the past. I wasn't going to allow myself to believe anything until it had actually happened. Given his record for making miraculous courtroom escapes, Billy Dunlop might still evade justice yet if we didn't stay doggedly on his trail till the last moment, till we finally heard a jury pronounce him 'guilty' and a judge say the word 'life'.

The one thing about Julie's murder that we still hadn't told Kevin was the fact that her vagina had been badly torn after she was dead. It was not a detail that had come out too much in the press and so we thought we could spare him that, at least for the moment. He'd had enough to take in already. To be honest it was a detail I found hard to even bring myself to think about, let alone talk about to my grandson, and I'm sure Andrew felt the same. The police, however, said that they believed if there was to be a re-trial what happened after Julie was dead would be bound to be brought up and since Kevin, now aged twenty, wanted to be in the courtroom they suggested he should be prepared in advance so that it didn't come as a complete shock. I could see what they meant. I could remember how shocked I was to hear about Julie's sex life for the first time in a public courtroom, and it seemed a terrible thing for a boy to have to hear about his mother.

It wasn't something any of us wanted to talk to him about ourselves, so a police liaison officer and our old friend Mark Braithwaite agreed to take Kevin away and have a chat to him. I was relieved. I thought it would be easier for him to hear it from them because they were less likely to become emotional about it and he would be able to ask them direct questions without worrying about upsetting them.

When he came back from the meeting Kevin was very quiet and obviously didn't want to talk about it any more. It was a lot for any boy to have to think about and we all left him alone to take his time. None of us were talking about the grimmest details unless we absolutely had to.

In May Charlie, Kevin and I went down to London with the police to attend the hearing about quashing the acquittal. I understood that once that was out of the way we were legally back to square one and they could set about trying Billy again as if none of the previous seventeen years had happened.

It had been six years since Charlie and I had seen Dunlop in the flesh and when we walked into the courtroom and saw him sitting in a big glass case we were shocked by how much weight he'd put on in prison. His thinning, greying hair was greasy and pulled back in a ponytail. His bloated face was even more immobile than before, if that was possible, showing no emotion, giving no clues as to what he might be thinking. The dangerous, bullying, self-styled hard man of a few years before had degenerated into a fat, middle-aged slob of a jailbird.

Although we were sitting only a few yards away from him he didn't look in our direction once throughout the proceedings. He must have expected us to be there because we were always there wherever he was taken but this time we were accompanied by Kevin, the boy he had deprived of a mother. His last memory of us would have been me flying across the courtroom towards him at the end of the perjury trial, shouting abuse and having to be restrained. I was calmer now, praying that I was about to see him brought to justice at last.

They had escorted him down for the hearing from Rampton Prison, a high security psychiatric hospital, which was originally built as an overflow for Broadmoor and housed a number of highly dangerous and violent psychopaths just like him. There were seven wardens standing around the glass case, ensuring that nothing could go wrong at this final stage. It was like a scene from a Hannibal Lecter film. Maybe they were protecting him from me as much as the other way round after the last time I flew at him.

The five distinguished law lords listened as the defending lawyer pleaded that had Dunlop known the law was going to change he would never have confessed. He claimed Billy had been encouraged to come clean by his barrister at the time. I couldn't see that any of what he was saying made any difference at all, but my heart was in my mouth the whole time for fear that he would say something that would influence the judges the wrong way. I tried to read from their expressions what they were thinking but it was impossible. Their wise-looking faces were just as inscrutable as Dunlop's or Charlie's; they weren't about to give anything away.

The prosecuting barrister said a few things in response after a short lunch break and then the judges all stood up and walked sedately out of the court, shutting the door firmly behind them. I assumed they were now going to tell us to come back in a fortnight, to hear their decision once they'd made their minds up. I prepared myself mentally for yet another delay. I had grown used to having to wait for everything; I could handle a couple more weeks as long as I got the result I wanted.

It seemed as though the judges couldn't have done more than stand outside and count to ten before the door opened again and they trooped solemnly back in, sat down and instantly quashed the acquittal. A stunned silence fell on the room at the announcement, everyone looking around at one another in disbelief. Even I was silenced. How could it have been so easy after such a long and hard struggle? Now Billy Dunlop could be tried once more for a murder he had already confessed to. Surely this time nothing else could go wrong? I watched as he was led out of the court by the guards but he didn't once look back at me.

The safeguards that had been put into place in the new law included an embargo on publicity during the retrial and stipulated that they had to be held at a different end of the country from the original trial. I suppose the thinking was that if there was a press outcry it could be said to prejudice the case and the whole thing would then be deemed a mistrial again. So the general public knew nothing about what was going on as we waited to be given a date for a retrial at the Old Bailey, Britain's Central Criminal Court in London. I lived in constant fear that something would go wrong with this new, untested retrial and Dunlop would end up being acquitted yet again on some minor technicality or other. Nothing like this had happened in England for at least 800 years so how could anyone predict how it would turn out?

When Ken MacDonald, the Director of Public Prosecutions asked to meet us again we returned to London with our hearts in our mouths, certain that something else must have gone wrong, that a new obstacle to us obtaining justice must have raised its head.

'We've had massive interest from abroad,' he told us once we were sitting down in his office. 'From Australia, New Zealand, America, the Caribbean, all the places that follow British law. Have you thought about writing a book?'

'Oh aye,' I said. 'It's in hand.' It was an idea I'd been considering on and off over the years but I'd decided I couldn't start writing until my story had an ending, until I had some kind of closure.

'Would you be mentioning people who helped you on your way?' he asked.

'You're skirting around the bushes here,' I said, 'but what you're really asking is can you have a mention in dispatches? Is that what you mean?'

'I suppose so,' he stuttered, 'yes.'

That, it seemed, was all the meeting had been about, so we headed back home feeling deeply relieved that it had proved to be a false alarm and that our fears had been raised for nothing. We were still on course for victory as long as nothing else went wrong at the last minute.

At his first appearance in the Old Bailey Dunlop pleaded 'not guilty', and my heart sank once more at the thought of having to sit through the whole trial for a third time, listening to them trying to drag Julie's name through the mud and having to relive inside my head those terrible moments inside the bathroom at 27 Grange Avenue. I couldn't understand how Dunlop

could be allowed to do that after he had already confessed so openly on tape and in court, but our barrister
explained that when he came back to court the next time
he would probably plead guilty.

'It's just a delaying tactic,' he said.

Sure enough on the second appearance Dunlop
changed his plea to 'guilty'.

I had waited so long to hear him actually saying that
word as an admission rather than a boast that it was hard
to believe my own ears. He spoke very quietly but the
word was clear enough. Now we didn't have to go
through another trial, we could go straight to the sentencing.

By the time Dunlop returned to the Old Bailey for
sentencing it was October 2006, just a month short of
seventeen years since Julie was killed. Jayne, his ex-girl-
friend and the mother of his three children, came down
to London at the request of the prosecutors because she
was a potential character witness. I can only imagine
what memories she must have of her time with him and
how fearful she must have been that he would ever be
released back into society, free to come knocking on her
door, demanding to see his kids.

'Jayne wants to have a chat with you,' the police told
me.

I couldn't see any harm in it. I certainly had nothing
against her and in many ways we had a lot in common.

I followed them into a little room where we could have a cup of tea and found her already sitting there. I was shocked by how much she had changed since I'd last seen her and it reminded me of just how many years of all our lives had been eaten up by the fight to bring Billy Dunlop to justice. I must have changed a lot myself during those seventeen years as well.

'In the end I had to leave him because he tried to strangle me,' she said once we were talking. 'As he was doing it he told me he would do the same to me that he'd done to Julie.'

She explained how she had eventually managed to get away from him, but only after years of horrendous abuse. She talked about the daughter she'd had with him and said that her boys were grown up now and that they hated their dad as much as she did for what he had done to Julie. As we were talking her phone rang and it was one of her lads. She told him she was with Julie's mam and he asked her to pass the phone over to me. I took it from her, not quite sure what to expect.

'I just want to apologize to you for what my father did to your daughter,' he said.

'You don't need to apologize,' I told him.

'He might be my father,' he said, 'but he's an animal.'

Jayne and I went on talking together for a while.

'I've been considering going to visit him in prison,' I told her. The idea had been growing in my head, but

I knew Charlie was strongly opposed to it so I hadn't done anything. 'Do you suppose if I wrote to him he would agree to see me?'

'I think he might, yes,' she said after a moment's thought. 'I'll tell you something; you're the only woman who's ever stood up to him in his life. Everyone else has always been scared stiff of him.'

She obviously didn't realize how scared I had been all those years when he had been out on the streets and I had laid awake in bed imagining him turning up at the front door the worse for drink and armed with God knows what.

When they told us it was time, we filed through into court number one and took our seats. This was it, the moment we had been fighting for over so many years. The judge came in and I tried to read from his face what he was likely to be saying but it was expressionless. Would he think that Billy had served enough years in prison and didn't need any more added to his sentence? Or would he decide to make an example of him, to show that no one was above the law? It was impossible to guess which way he would go. Eventually everything settled down in the room and the moment had arrived.

Billy Dunlop sat silently in the dock and listened as the judge read out parts of our impact statement. I liked the idea that he was being forced to listen to someone else telling him a bit of what he had put us through over the years. At the end the judge announced that Dunlop was to receive a life sentence, with a seventeen-year tariff before he could apply for parole, which I knew was a long tariff. The judge was showing that he agreed with us that Billy should be made to pay the full price for what he did to our daughter, even if it had happened seventeen years before.

At last we had got justice for Julie. After all the waiting and all the fighting and all the heartbreak I had finally heard a judge pronounce the word 'life' on Billy Dunlop for what he did to all of us that night in 1989. I stared hard at him but he didn't look surprised or upset. He didn't turn to look at any of us watching; he was as emotionless as always.

It took a while for the full impact of what had happened to sink into my brain. The first man in Britain to be re-tried for a crime in 800 years had been found guilty and sentenced. History had been made. I was in a daze, not sure if I was going to laugh or cry as we were led from the courtroom and steered back towards the street. I thanked the barrister, Andrew Robertson QC.

'You don't need to thank me,' he said kindly. 'It's the whole of the Establishment who need to thank you for your campaign.'

When we emerged from the gates of the Old Bailey it looked as though the whole of the world's press was waiting for us outside. There were so many of them the police had had to close the road. It seemed that Ken Macdonald had been right and the law of double jeopardy was of interest to a lot of other countries that modelled their legal systems on the British one. I wished I'd been given a few minutes' warning so I could have composed myself before I was brought out into this barrage of noise and cameras at a moment when I was feeling so many emotions at once.

'How do you feel?' I heard someone ask amidst the explosion of questions and shouting voices coming at us from every direction.

I actually felt like jumping up in the air and shouting 'Justice for Julie, at last!' I felt that after all the fighting and all the stress and all the knock-backs that my little girl, who had arrived into the world like an angel, could now rest in peace knowing that her killer was behind bars for what he did to her that night. We had created a lasting legacy for her and Charlie had carried out the promise he made to her that day in the funeral parlour when he lay across her coffin to talk to her for the last time.

Once it was all over the police asked us if we would like to hear the tape of Dunlop's confession. I don't know why we agreed to do it – maybe because we thought it would give us some closure, or maybe because we were in a bit of a daze and did whatever anyone suggested.

I think with hindsight that the police wanted us to hear it privately before excerpts of it were broadcast to the rest of the world.

It felt strange to hear his voice actually talking about what he had done, making real all the images that had been travelling around in my imagination for so long. In his version of the story he told them that he had killed her about an hour after arriving at the house, which would have made it around ten past three, the moment that I woke up at home with a terrible feeling inside me and thought about calling Julie. The thought sent a shudder through me.

Now that it is all over I do feel I might be able to visit Dunlop in prison and actually ask him to explain why he did what he did. I don't believe that he entered that house with the intention of killing anyone, so I just want him to look me in the eye and make me understand what happened. I don't believe his story that he killed her just because she laughed at his black eye. I want him to tell me about her last moments of life. Of course, he might not answer my questions. He might be unhelpful and sullen or even threatening. But hearing the story in his own words might help me, I think.

Charlie still doesn't agree with the idea of going to see him because he says we wouldn't be able to believe anything Dunlop said anyway, and I can see what he means. I don't know if I would believe him or not.

I had a dream a couple of years ago where I found myself back in Blackpool Tower Ballroom. I was in a disco, watching a crowd of people dancing under one of those big silver balls that reflect all the lights. The music was loud and the dance floor was packed. In the middle of the crowd I could see Julie, dancing like she used to, wearing a bright turquoise dress. She was always such a good dancer. I felt relieved to see she hadn't been murdered at all, that she was there in front of me. I pushed my way through, parting the gyrating crowd as I went.

'You've never been murdered,' I said when I got to her. 'You're all right.'

'Been murdered?' she said, not stopping her dancing. 'What do you mean, been murdered?'

I grabbed hold of her skinny arm and I could feel every bone in her and I knew for sure she was alive.

When I woke up my first thought was that I'd had a terrible dream about Julie having been murdered. For a split second I thought the scene on the dance floor had been the reality and that she was all right, but then the truth all came rushing back and the sadness returned. I guess having a dream like that must mean I've travelled on a long way from the years when my mind was trapped under that bath, just as Julie's body was. But Julie will never travel on anywhere now. While Charlie and I have grown old and her brother and sister have become middle-aged, she is still that 22-year-old girl, whirling around the dance floor in a turquoise dress without a care in the world. I sometimes wonder if she will still look like that if we are allowed to meet in the afterlife.

People often ask me if I have ever 'seen' Julie since her death, knowing that I believe strongly in that sort of thing, but I have to tell them I haven't. Charlie believes he has, and I know she is still there inside both our heads somewhere, but I would love to see her again, even if it was only as a visitor from the spirit world.

I was giving a talk to a group of trainee bereavement counsellors once and an Indian woman in the audience was waiting to have a word with me as I came out.

'I hope you don't mind me saying,' she said, 'but all the time you were doing your talk your daughter was stood beside you. She's really proud of what you've achieved. She said "Just say to our Mam that I'm holding a bunch of pink carnations."'

Pink carnations were our Julie's favourite flower so that was a very moving moment.

I like dancing myself and recently I've taken up line dancing. It takes me out of myself and gives me a chance to meet people who know nothing about murder cases or double jeopardy laws, although everyone in the group was very supportive and gave me some lovely flowers when the law changed. For the two hours we are dancing I don't have to think about anything except the steps and the music. I still need to keep myself busy, even now, to keep my mind distracted.

If I'm sitting on my own doing nothing I tend to find myself getting out all the sympathy cards and letters we've received over the years and I read through them and have a really good cry, just like that vicar we heard about with the picture of his daughter and the ballet music on the stereo system. Then after a while I feel better and put them back in their drawer.

I have a blouse that belonged to Julie, which I keep rolled up in a drawer, and every so often I take it out and press my face into the material, breathing in the scent. It doesn't smell of Julie herself any more but it still brings back the memories. It's the only piece of her clothing that I kept when Angela cleared all the rest out. From what I can understand I think all bereaved mothers do something like that.

The Chief Constable wrote recently to tell me I had won a 'good citizen award'. He wrote: 'Your actions following the death of your daughter, your determination in helping to secure the successful conviction of William

Vincent Dunlop for murder have been remarkable. This investigation has literally changed the course of British legal history.' It seems a long way from the days when men in positions like his wouldn't even come to talk to us.

At about the same time I got a letter from the Cabinet Secretary at 10 Downing Street, telling me I was going to be awarded an MBE. I thought it was a joke at first but it wasn't. In October 2007 I went to Buckingham Palace and received my award from Prince Charles. He was very compassionate and said to me that I'd done a 'splendid job', adding that hopefully I would get some form of closure now.

When the case was all over and I was sitting at home being interviewed for another documentary, the producer asked me what I thought Julie would say if she was watching from the other side. I thought for a second.

'I think,' I told him, 'she'd say "Well done, our Mam."'

Epilogue

Whenever we walk around Billingham town centre, even today, so many people still come up and tell me they support us and congratulate us on what we have achieved. Sometimes we end up with quite a crowd round us.

It's nice to have succeeded in what we set out to do, but I'm still angry. I can't pretend I'm not. I'm angry with Billy Dunlop for what he did to Julie and angry with the police for making such a mess of everything in the beginning, causing us so many years of extra agony and struggle when we should have been allowed time to recover from the pain of losing our daughter.

I'm still doing my talks to police training courses in West Yorkshire and at the National Police Training centre down in St Neots, trying to give them an insight into what it's like being on the other side of the fence in an investigation. I talk to family liaison officers, telling them our story and answering questions, and I do another course for superintendents. The police trainers actually use a video of our story as a case study of 'how not to search a house'.

Having said all that, if the police had found her body within those first few days Dunlop would almost certainly have been convicted and the maximum sentence then for murder was twelve years, so he would have been back on the streets years ago. I would also never have heard of the law of double jeopardy, and who knows if it would have been changed yet without the extra pressure of Julie's case? So maybe everything really does happen for a reason.

Because of all that went wrong we got a chance to make a little bit of history, but that still doesn't bring our Julie back. Nothing will.

Kevin has left home now and is living with his partner, Amber. His mum would be so proud of him. I see and speak to him all the time, just as I used to see Julie. He's in and out of the house for cups of tea and chats, and he's a really good support to Charlie and me.

Gary is married with a family and Angela has a boy and a girl. Her daughter Emily is twelve now and physically she could be a reincarnation of Julie. She's not quite as dark but she has a certain look about her that's like my beautiful daughter all over again. She was stir-frying something in the kitchen the other day and turned to me and I almost jumped with shock at the strong resemblance.

You can't ever turn the clock back, but at last I can look into the future again after all those years fighting for justice. I can move forwards and help my grandchildren to make happy lives for themselves, and I can look after Charlie as we both get older. I'll keep doing my talks to the police, because it's good to feel I can make a bit of a difference, but I doubt I'll be taking on any more campaigns again. I'm all campaigned out now!